to

_____

from

_____

2minutes

A DAY

100 DEVOTIONALS

for girls

Scripture quotations are taken from:

The Holy Bible, King James Version

The Holy Bible, New International Version (NIV) Copyright © 1973, 1978, 1984, by International Bible Society. Used by permission of Zondervan Publishing House. All rights reserved.

The New American Standard Bible®, (NASB) Copyright © 1960, 1962, 1963, 1968, 1971, 1972, 1973, 1975, 1977, 1995 by The Lockman Foundation. Used by permission.

The Holy Bible, New King James Version (NKJV) Copyright © 1982 by Thomas Nelson, Inc. Used by permission.

The Holy Bible, New Living Translation, (NLT) Copyright © 1996. Used by permission of Tyndale House Publishers, Inc., Wheaton, Illinois 60189. All rights reserved.

New Century Version®. (NCV) Copyright © 1987, 1988, 1991 by Word Publishing, a division of Thomas Nelson, Inc. All rights reserved. Used by permission.

The Holy Bible: Revised Standard Version (RSV). Copyright 1946, 1952, 1959, 1973 by the Division of Christian Education of the National Council of the Churches of Christ in the United States of America. All rights reserved. Used by permission.

The Holy Bible, The Living Bible (TLB), Copyright © 1971 owned by assignment by Illinois Regional Bank N.A. (as trustee). Used by permission of Tyndale House Publishers, Inc., Wheaton, Illinois 60189. All rights reserved.

The Message (MSG) This edition issued by contractual arrangement with NavPress, a division of The Navigators, U.S.A. Originally published by NavPress in English as THE MESSAGE: The Bible in Contemporary Language copyright 2002-2003 by Eugene Peterson. All rights reserved.

The Holman Christian Standard Bible™ (HCSB) Copyright © 1999, 2000, 2001 by Holman Bible Publishers. Used by permission.

Cover Design by Kim Russell / Wahoo Designs
Page Layout by Bart Dawson

ISBN 1-58334-319-9

ISBN-13 978-1-58334-319-7

2minutes A DAY

100 DEVOTIONALS for girls

Introduction

Can you spare two minutes each day for God? Of course you can . . . and of course you should! No matter how busy you are, you should never allow the stresses of everyday living to come between you and your Creator.

As you know from firsthand experience, it isn't easy being a young woman in our 21st-century world. Every day, you are confronted with countless opportunities to wander far from the path that God intends for your life. Every day, you come face-to-face with temptations and distractions that were unknown to previous generations. Every day, you have difficult choices to make—choices that can quite literally affect the rest of your life. And, the world is changing so rapidly that, at times, it seems difficult to catch your breath and keep your balance. This little book is intended to help.

This book contains 100 brief devotional readings of particular interest to young women like you. Each chapter contains a Bible verse, a short essay, quotations from noted Christian women (plus quotes from a few men, too), and a prayer.

Are you facing difficult decisions? Are you seeking to change some aspect of your life? Do you desire the eternal abundance and peace that can be yours through Christ? If so, ask for God's help and ask for it many times each day . . . starting with a regular, heartfelt morning devotional. Even two minutes is enough time to change your day . . . and your life.

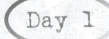

Who's First?

Do not worship any other gods besides me.

EXODUS 20:3 NLT

Who is in charge of your heart? Is it God, or is it something else? Have you given Christ your heart, your soul, your talents, your time, and your testimony? Or are you giving Him little more than a few hours each Sunday morning?

In the book of Exodus, God warns that we should place no gods before Him. Yet all too often, we place our Lord in second, third, or fourth place as we worship other things. When we unwittingly place possessions or relationships above our love for the Creator, we create big problems for ourselves.

Does God rule your heart? Make certain that the honest answer to this question is a resounding yes. In the life of every radical believer, God comes first. And that's precisely the place that He deserves in your heart.

more stuff to think about

When all else is gone, God is still left.
Nothing changes Him.

HANNAH WHITALL SMITH

To God be the glory, great things He has done;
So loved He the world that He gave us His Son.

FANNY CROSBY

Today's Prayer

Dear Lord, Your power, like Your love, is infinite. I thank You, Father, for the gift of eternal life through the sacrifice of Your Son Jesus. I will keep the promise of heaven fresh in my heart. And, while I am in this world, I will pass through it with praise on my lips and love in my heart for You. Amen

for girls

The Power of Perseverance

I have fought the good fight, I have finished the race,
I have kept the faith.

2 TIMOTHY 4:7 NIV

A well-lived life is like a marathon, not a sprint—it calls for preparation, determination, and, of course, lots of perseverance. As an example of perfect perseverance, we Christians need look no further than our Savior, Jesus Christ.

Jesus finished what He began. Despite His suffering, despite the shame of the cross, Jesus was steadfast in His faithfulness to God. We, too, must remain faithful, especially during times of hardship. Sometimes, God may answer our prayers with silence, and when He does, we must patiently persevere.

Are you facing a tough situation? If so, remember this: whatever your problem, God can handle it. Your job is to keep persevering until He does.

When you fall and skin your knees and skin your heart,
He'll pick you up.

CHARLES STANLEY

Failure is one of life's most powerful teachers.
How we handle our failures determines whether
we're going to simply "get by" in life or "press on."

BETH MOORE

Today's Prayer

Dear Lord, when I'm discouraged—or worse—let me
turn to You for strength, for courage, and for love. Let
me trust You completely, today and forever. Amen

for girls

The Best Policy

The honest person will live in safety,
but the dishonest will be caught.

PROVERBS 10:9 NCV

It has been said on many occasions and in many ways that honesty is the best policy. For believers, it is far more important to note that honesty is God's policy. And if we are to be servants worthy of our Savior, Jesus Christ, we must be honest and forthright in our communications with others.

Sometimes, honesty is difficult; sometimes, honesty is painful; always, honesty is God's commandment. In the Book of Exodus, God did not command, "Thou shalt not bear false witness when it is convenient." And He didn't say, "Thou shalt not bear false witness most of the time." God said, "Thou shalt not bear false witness against thy neighbor." Period.

Sometime soon, perhaps even today, you will be tempted to bend the truth or perhaps even to break it. Resist that temptation. Truth is God's way…and it must also be yours. Period.

more stuff to think about

The single most important element in any human relationship is honesty—with oneself, with God, and with others.

CATHERINE MARSHALL

Much guilt arises in the life of the believer from practicing the chameleon life of environmental adaptation.

BETH MOORE

Today's Prayer

Lord, sometimes it's hard to tell the truth. But even when telling the truth is difficult, let me follow Your commandment. Honesty isn't just the best policy, Lord; it's Your policy, and I will obey You by making it my policy, too. Amen

for girls

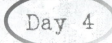

Day 4

Taking Time to Say "Thanks"

You are my God, and I will give you thanks; you are my God,
and I will exalt you. Give thanks to the LORD,
for he is good; his love endures forever.

PSALM 118:28-29 NIV

If you're like most females on the planet, you're a very busy girl. Your life is probably hectic, demanding, and complicated. When the demands of life leave you rushing from place to place with scarcely a moment to spare, you may fail to pause and thank your Creator for the blessings He has bestowed upon you. Big mistake.

No matter how busy you are, you should never be too busy to thank God for His gifts. Your task, as an extreme follower of the living Christ, is to praise God many times each day. Then, with gratitude in your heart, you can face your daily duties with the perspective and power that only He can provide.

When you slow down and express your gratitude to your Heavenly Father, you enrich your own life and the lives of those around you. That's why thanksgiving should become a habit, a regular part of your daily routine. Yes, God has blessed you beyond measure, and you owe Him everything, including your eternal praise.

more stuff to think about

It is always possible to be thankful for what is given rather than to complain about what is not given.
One or the other becomes a habit of life.

ELISABETH ELLIOT

God is in control, and therefore in everything I can give thanks, not because of the situation, but because of the One who directs and rules over it.

KAY ARTHUR

Today's Prayer

Lord, let me be a thankful Christian. Your blessings are priceless and eternal. I praise You, Lord, for Your gifts and, most of all, for Your Son. Amen

for girls

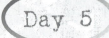

The Wisdom Not to Judge

Do not judge, or you too will be judged.
For in the same way you judge others, you will be judged,
and with the measure you use,
it will be measured to you.

MATTHEW 7:1 NIV

Here's something worth thinking about: If you judge other people harshly, God will judge you in the same fashion. But that's not all (thank goodness!). The Bible also promises that if you forgive others, you, too, will be forgiven.

Have you developed the bad habit of behaving yourself like an amateur judge and jury, assigning blame and condemnation wherever you go? If so, it's time to grow up and obey God. When it comes to judging everything and everybody, God doesn't need your help . . . and He doesn't want it.

more stuff to think about

Judging draws the judgment of others.

CATHERINE MARSHALL

No creed or school of thought can monopolize
the Spirit of God.

OSWALD CHAMBERS

Today's Prayer

Lord, You know that I can size up others very quickly.
And, I can be very wrong. Help me not to judge. I only
see a little, but You see the whole. You are the One who
searches the heart and knows everything about all of
us. You love all Your children, Lord, and so should I.
Amen

for girls

The Right Crowd

*Greater love has no one than this,
that he lay down his life for his friends.*

JOHN 15:13 NIV

Are you hanging out with people who make you a better Christian, or are you spending time with people who encourage you to stray from your faith? The answer to this question will have a surprising impact on the condition of your spiritual health.

Our world is filled with pressures: some good, some bad. The pressures that we feel to follow God's will and obey His commandments are positive pressures. God places them on our hearts so that we might act in accordance with His will. But we also face different pressures, ones that are definitely not from God. When we feel pressured to do things—or even to think thoughts—that lead us away from Him, we must beware.

If we are to please God, we must resist the pressures that society seeks to impose upon us, and we must conform ourselves, instead, to His will, to His path, and to His Son.

more stuff to think about

Perhaps the greatest treasure on earth and one of the
only things that will survive this life is human relationships:
old friends. We are indeed rich if we have friends.
Friends who have loved us through the problems and
heartaches of life. Deep, true, joyful friendships.
Life is too short and eternity too long to live
without old friends.

GLORIA GAITHER

The glory of friendship is not the outstretched hand,
or the kindly smile, or the joy of companionship.
It is the spiritual inspiration that comes to one when
he discovers that someone else believes in him and
is willing to trust him with his friendship.

CORRIE TEN BOOM

Today's Prayer

Lord, thank You for my friends. Let me be a
trustworthy friend to others, and let my love for You be
reflected in my genuine love for them. Amen

for girls

Healthy Habits

Do not be deceived: "Evil company corrupts good habits."
1 CORINTHIANS 15:33 NKJV

It's an old saying and a true one: First, you make your habits, and then your habits make you. Some habits will inevitably bring you closer to God; other habits will lead you away from the path He has chosen for you. If you sincerely desire to improve your spiritual health, you must honestly examine the habits that make up the fabric of your day. And you must abandon those habits that are displeasing to God.

If you trust God, and if you keep asking for His help, He can transform your life. If you sincerely ask Him to help you, the same God who created the universe will help you defeat the harmful habits that have heretofore defeated you. So, if at first you don't succeed, keep praying. God is listening, and He's ready to help you become a better person if you ask Him . . . so ask today.

more stuff to think about

Since behaviors become habits,
make them work with you and not against you.

E. STANLEY JONES

You will never change your life until you change
something you do daily.

JOHN MAXWELL

Today's Prayer

Dear Lord, help me break bad habits and form good
ones. And let my actions be pleasing to You, today and
every day. Amen

Day 8

Imitating Christ

*Watch what God does, and then you do it, like children
who learn proper behavior from their parents. Mostly what
God does is love you. Keep company with him and
learn a life of love. Observe how Christ loved us.
His love was not cautious but extravagant.*

EPHESIANS 5:1-2 MSG

Imitating Christ is impossible, but attempting to imitate Him is both possible and advisable. By attempting to imitate Jesus, we seek, to the best of our abilities, to walk in His footsteps. To the extent we succeed in following Him, we receive the spiritual abundance that is the rightful possession of those who love Christ and keep His commandments.

Do you seek God's blessings for the day ahead? Then, to the best of your abilities, imitate His Son. You will fall short, of course. But if your heart is right and your intentions are pure, God will bless your efforts, your day, and your life.

2 MINUTES A DAY

more stuff to think about

You cannot cooperate with Jesus in becoming what He wants you to become and simultaneously be what the world desires to make you. If you would say, "Take the world but give me Jesus," then you must deny yourself and take up your cross. The simple truth is that your "self" must be put to death in order for you to get to the point where for you to live is Christ. What will it be? The world and you, or Jesus and you? You do have a choice to make.

KAY ARTHUR

Every Christian is to become a little Christ. The whole purpose of becoming a Christian is simply nothing else.

C. S. LEWIS

Today's Prayer

Dear Lord, You sent Your Son so that I might have abundant life and eternal life. Thank You, Father, for my Savior, Christ Jesus. I will follow Him, honor Him, and share His Good News, this day and every day. Amen

for girls

So Laugh!

There is a time for everything, and everything on earth has its special season. There is a time to cry and a time to laugh. There is a time to be sad and a time to dance.

ECCLESIASTES 3:1,4 NCV

Laughter is a gift from God, a gift that He intends for us to use. Yet sometimes, because of the inevitable stresses of everyday living, we fail to find the fun in life. When we allow life's inevitable disappointments to cast a pall over our lives and our souls, we do a profound disservice to ourselves and to our loved ones.

If you've allowed the clouds of life to obscure the blessings of life, perhaps you've formed the unfortunate habit of taking things just a little too seriously. If so, it's time to fret a little less and laugh a little more.

So today, look for the humor that most certainly surrounds you—when you do, you'll find it. And remember: God created laughter for a reason…and Father indeed knows best. So laugh!

more stuff to think about

I want to encourage you in these days with
your family to lighten up and enjoy.
Laugh a little bit; it might just set you free.

DENNIS SWANBERG

He who laughs lasts—he who doesn't, doesn't.

MARIE T. FREEMAN

Today's Prayer

Dear Lord, laughter is Your gift to me; help me to enjoy
it. Today and every day, put a smile on my face, and
help me to share that smile with other people, starting
with my family. This is the day that You have made,
Lord. Let me enjoy it . . . and let me laugh. Amen

for girls

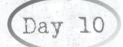

Quiet Time with God

Knowing God leads to self-control.
Self-control leads to patient endurance,
and patient endurance leads to godliness.
2 PETER 1:6 NLT

Do you ever wonder if God is really "right here, right now"? Do you wonder if God hears your prayers, if He understands your feelings, or if He really knows your heart? If so, you're not alone: lots of very faithful Christians have experienced periods of doubt. In fact, some of the biggest heroes in the Bible had plenty of doubts—and so, perhaps, will you. But when you have doubts, remember this: God isn't on a coffee break, and He hasn't moved out of town. God isn't taking a long vacation, and He isn't snoozing on the couch. He's right here, right now, listening to your thoughts and prayers, watching over your every move.

When you quiet yourself and acknowledge His presence, God touches your heart and restores your spirits. So why not let Him do it right now? If you really want to know Him better, silence is a wonderful place to start.

more stuff to think about

You cannot grow spiritually until you have
the assurance that Christ is in your life.

VONETTE BRIGHT

Here is our opportunity: we cannot see God,
but we can see Christ. Christ was not only the Son of God,
but He was the Father. Whatever Christ was, that God is.

HANNAH WHITALL SMITH

Today's Prayer

Dear Lord, help me remember the importance of silence.
Help me discover quiet moments throughout the day so
that I can sense Your presence and Your love. Amen

for girls

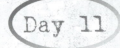

God's Timetable

He has made everything beautiful in its time.
He has also set eternity in the hearts of men;
yet they cannot fathom what God has done
from beginning to end.

ECCLESIASTES 3:11 NIV

Are you anxious for God to work out His plan for your life? Who isn't? As believers, we all want God to do great things for us and through us, and we want Him to do those things now. But sometimes, God has other plans. Sometimes, God's timetable does not coincide with our own. It's worth noting, however, that God's timetable is always perfect.

The next time you find your patience tested to the limit, remember that the world unfolds according to God's plan, not ours. Sometimes, we must wait patiently, and that's as it should be. After all, think how patient God has been with us.

more stuff to think about

When there is perplexity there is always guidance—
not always at the moment we ask, but in good time,
which is God's time. There is no need to fret and stew.

ELISABETH ELLIOT

Your times are in His hands.
He's in charge of the timetable, so wait patiently.

KAY ARTHUR

Today's Prayer

Lord, my sense of timing is fallible and imperfect;
Yours is not. Let me trust in Your timetable for my
life, and give me the patience and the wisdom to trust
Your plans, not my own. Amen

for girls

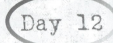

Listening to God

The one who is from God listens to God's words.
This is why you don't listen, because you are not from God.
JOHN 8:47 HCSB

Sometimes God speaks loudly and clearly. More often, He speaks in a quiet voice—and if you are wise, you will be listening carefully when He does. To do so, you must carve out quiet moments each day to study His Word and sense His direction.

Can you quiet yourself long enough to listen to your conscience? Are you attuned to the subtle guidance of your intuition? Are you willing to pray sincerely and then to wait quietly for God's response? Hopefully so. Usually God refrains from sending His messages on stone tablets or city billboards. More often, He communicates in subtler ways. If you sincerely desire to hear His voice, you must listen carefully, and you must do so in the silent corners of your quiet, willing heart.

more stuff to think about

When we come to Jesus stripped of pretensions,
with a needy spirit, ready to listen,
He meets us at the point of need.

CATHERINE MARSHALL

God is always listening.

STORMIE OMARTIAN

Today's Prayer

Heavenly Father, in these quiet moments before this
busy day unfolds, I come to You. May my meditations
bring You pleasure just as surely as they bring me a
clearer sense of Your love and Your peace. May the time
I spend in quiet meditation mold my day and my
life...for You. Amen

for girls

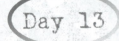

Do You Believe in Miracles?

With God's power working in us, God can do much, much more than anything we can ask or imagine.
EPHESIANS 3:20 NCV

D o you believe that God is at work in the world? And do you also believe that nothing is impossible for Him? If so, then you also believe that God is perfectly capable of doing things that you, as a mere human being with limited vision and limited understanding, would deem to be utterly impossible. And that's precisely what God does.

Since the moment that He created our universe out of nothingness, God has made a habit of doing miraculous things. And He still works miracles today. Expect Him to work miracles in your own life, and then be watchful. With God, absolutely nothing is impossible, including an amazing assortment of miracles that He stands ready, willing, and able to perform for you and yours.

more stuff to think about

I could go through this day oblivious to the miracles
all around me or I could tune in and "enjoy."

GLORIA GAITHER

God specializes in things thought impossible.

CATHERINE MARSHALL

Today's Prayer

Lord, for You, nothing is impossible. Let me trust in
Your power to do the miraculous, and let me trust in
Your willingness to work miracles in my life—and in
my heart. Amen

for girls

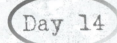

When People Are Cruel

Kind people do themselves a favor,
but cruel people bring trouble on themselves.
PROVERBS 11:17 NCV

Face it: sometimes people can be cruel . . . very cruel. When other people are unkind to you or to your friends, you may be tempted to strike back, either verbally or in some other way. Don't do it! Instead, remember that God corrects other people's behaviors in His own way, and He doesn't need your help (even if you're totally convinced that He does!). Remember that God has commanded you to forgive others, just as you, too, must sometimes seek forgiveness from others.

So, when other people behave cruelly, foolishly, or impulsively—as they will from time to time—don't be a hotheaded girl. Instead, speak up for yourself as politely as you can, and walk away. Then, forgive everybody as quickly as you can, and leave the rest up to God.

You can be sure you are abiding in Christ
if you are able to have a Christlike love toward the people
that irritate you the most.

VONETTE BRIGHT

A keen sense of humor helps us to overlook
the unbecoming, understand the unconventional,
tolerate the unpleasant, overcome the unexpected,
and outlast the unbearable.

BILLY GRAHAM

Today's Prayer

Heavenly Father, make me a kind person even to those
who don't treat me kindly. Let me forgive others, just
as you have forgiven me. Amen

for girls

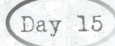

Beyond Fear

Even when I walk through the dark valley of death,
I will not be afraid, for you are close beside me.
Your rod and your staff protect and comfort me.

PSALM 23:4 NLT

We live in a world that is, at times, a frightening place. We live in a world that is, at times, a discouraging place. We live in a world where life-changing losses can be so painful and so profound that it seems we will never recover. But, with God's help, and with the help of encouraging family members and friends, we can recover.

During the darker days of life, we are wise to remember the words of Jesus, who reassured His disciples, saying, "Take courage! It is I. Don't be afraid" (Matthew 14:27 NIV). Then, with God's comfort and His love in our hearts, we can offer encouragement to others. And by helping them face their fears, we can, in turn, tackle our own problems with courage, determination, and faith.

more stuff to think about

Worry is a cycle of inefficient thoughts whirling
around a center of fear.

CORRIE TEN BOOM

When once we are assured that God is good,
then there can be nothing left to fear.

HANNAH WHITALL SMITH

Today's Prayer

Dear Lord, when I am fearful, keep me mindful that
You are my protector and my salvation. Thank You,
Father, for a perfect love that casts out fear. Because of
You, I can live courageously and faithfully this day
and every day. Amen

for girls

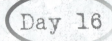

God's Gifts to You

Each one has his own gift from God,
one in this manner and another in that.

1 CORINTHIANS 7:7 NKJV

Face it: you've got an array of talents that need to be refined. All people possess special gifts—bestowed from the Father above—and you are no exception. But, your gift is no guarantee of success; it must be cultivated—by you—or it will go unused . . . and God's gift to you will be squandered.

Today, make a promise to yourself that you will earnestly seek to discover the talents that God has given you. Then, nourish those talents and make them grow. Finally, vow to share your gifts with the world for as long as God gives you the power to do so. After all, the best way to say "Thank You" for God's gifts is to use them.

more stuff to think about

The Lord has abundantly blessed me all of my life.
I'm not trying to pay Him back for all of His wonderful gifts;
I just realize that He gave them to me to give away.

LISA WHELCHEL

God has given you special talents—now it's your turn
to give them back to God.

MARIE T. FREEMAN

Today's Prayer

Lord, I praise You for Your priceless gifts. I give thanks
for Your creation, for Your Son, and for the unique
talents and opportunities that You have given me. Let
me use my gifts for the glory of Your kingdom, this
day and every day. Amen

for girls

Optimistic Christianity

*My cup runs over. Surely goodness and mercy shall follow
me all the days of my life; and I will dwell in
the house of the Lord Forever.*

PSALM 23:5-6 NKJV

Face facts: pessimism and Christianity don't mix. Why? Because Christians have every reason to be optimistic about life here on earth and life eternal. Mrs. Charles E. Cowman advised, "Never yield to gloomy anticipation. Place your hope and confidence in God. He has no record of failure."

Today, make this promise to yourself and keep it: vow to be a hope-filled Christian. Think optimistically about your life, your education, your family, and your future. Trust your hopes, not your fears. Take time to celebrate God's glorious creation. And then, when you've filled your heart with hope, share your optimism with others. They'll be better for it, and so will you. But not necessarily in that order.

more stuff to think about

The Christian lifestyle is not one of legalistic do's and don'ts, but one that is positive, attractive, and joyful.

VONETTE BRIGHT

If you can't tell whether your glass is half-empty or half-full, you don't need another glass; what you need is better eyesight . . . and a more thankful heart.

MARIE T. FREEMAN

Today's Prayer

Dear Lord, I will look for the best in other people, I will expect the best from You, and I will try my best to do my best—today and every day. Amen

for girls

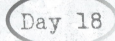

Making Peace with the Past

The Lord says, "Forget what happened before, and do not think about the past. Look at the new thing I am going to do. It is already happening. Don't you see it? I will make a road in the desert and rivers in the dry land."

Isaiah 43:18-19 NCV

Have you made peace with your past? If so, congratulations. But, if you are mired in the quicksand of regret, it's time to plan your escape. How can you do so? By accepting what has been and by trusting God for what will be.

Because you are human, you may be slow to forget yesterday's disappointments; if so, you are not alone. But if you sincerely seek to focus your hopes and energies on the future, then you must find ways to accept the past, no matter how difficult it may be to do so.

If you have not yet made peace with the past, today is the day to declare an end to all hostilities. When you do, you can then turn your thoughts to the wondrous promises of God and to the glorious future that He has in store for you.

more stuff to think about

Whoever you are, whatever your condition or circumstance,
whatever your past or problem,
Jesus can restore you to wholeness.

ANNE GRAHAM LOTZ

Shake the dust from your past,
and move forward in His promises.

KAY ARTHUR

Today's Prayer

Heavenly Father, free me from anger, resentment, and envy. When I am bitter, I cannot feel the peace that You intend for my life. Keep me mindful that forgiveness is Your commandment, and help me accept the past, treasure the present, and trust the future . . . to You. Amen

Your Bright Future

"I say this because I know what I am planning for you,"
says the Lord. "I have good plans for you, not plans to hurt
you. I will give you hope and a good future."
JEREMIAH 29:11 NCV

Let's talk for a minute about the future . . . your future. How bright do you believe your future to be? Well, if you're a faithful believer, God has plans for you that are so bright that you'd better pack several pairs of sunglasses and a lifetime supply of sunblock!

The way that you think about your future will play a powerful role in determining how things turn out (it's called the "self-fulfilling prophecy", and it applies to everybody, including you). So here's another question: Are you expecting a terrific tomorrow, or are you dreading a terrible one? The answer to that question will have a powerful impact on the way tomorrow unfolds.

Today, as you live in the present and look to the future, remember that God has an amazing plan for you. Act—and believe—accordingly. And one more thing: don't forget the sunblock.

more stuff to think about

Joy comes from knowing God loves me and knows
who I am and where I'm going . . .
that my future is secure as I rest in Him.

JAMES DOBSON

Do not limit the limitless God! With Him,
face the future unafraid because you are never alone.

MRS. CHARLES E. COWMAN

Today's Prayer

Lord, sometimes when I think about the future, I worry.
Today, I will do a better job of trusting You. If I become
discouraged, I will turn to You. If I am afraid, I will
seek strength in You. You are my Father, and I will
place my hope, my trust, and my faith in You. Amen

for girls

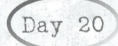

Sharing His Peace

And the peace of God, which surpasses all comprehension,
will guard your hearts and your minds in Christ Jesus.

Philippians 4:7 NASB

When we accept the peace of Jesus Christ into our hearts, our lives are transformed. And then, because we possess the gift of peace, we can share that gift with fellow Christians, family members, friends, and associates. If, on the other hand, we choose to ignore the gift of peace—for whatever reason—we cannot share what we do not possess.

As every young woman knows, peace can be a scarce commodity in a demanding, 21st-Century world. How, then, can we find the peace that we so desperately desire? By turning our days and our lives over to God. Elisabeth Elliot writes, "If my life is surrendered to God, all is well. Let me not grab it back, as though it were in peril in His hand but would be safer in mine!" May we give our lives, our hopes, and our prayers to the Lord, and, by doing so, accept His will and His peace.

more stuff to think about

God's peace is like a river, not a pond. In other words,
a sense of health and well-being, both of which are
expressions of the Hebrew shalom, can permeate
our homes even when we're in white-water rapids.

BETH MOORE

The fruit of our placing all things in God's hands is the
presence of His abiding peace in our hearts.

HANNAH WHITALL SMITH

Today's Prayer

Dear Lord, I will open my heart to You. And I thank
You, God, for Your love, for Your peace, and for Your
Son. Amen

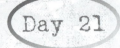

Choices

But Daniel purposed in his heart that he would not defile himself....

DANIEL 1:8 KJV

Your life is a series of choices. From the instant you wake up in the morning until the moment you nod off to sleep at night, you make lots of decisions: decisions about the things you do, decisions about the words you speak, and decisions about the thoughts you choose to think. Simply put, the quality of those decisions determines the quality of your life.

So, if you sincerely want to lead a life that is pleasing to God, you must make choices that are pleasing to Him. And you know what? He deserves no less . . . and neither, for that matter, do you.

more stuff to think about

God is voting for us all the time.
The devil is voting against us all the time.
The way we vote carries the election.

<small>CORRIE TEN BOOM</small>

Faith is not a feeling; it is action. It is a willed choice.

<small>ELISABETH ELLIOT</small>

Today's Prayer

Lord, help me to make choices that are pleasing to You.
Help me to be honest, patient, and kind. And above all,
help me to follow the teachings of Jesus, not just today,
but every day. Amen

Considering the Cross

But God forbid that I should boast except in the cross of our Lord Jesus Christ, by whom the world has been crucified to me, and I to the world.

GALATIANS 6:14 NKJV

As we consider Christ's sacrifice on the cross, we should be profoundly humbled and profoundly grateful. And today, as we come to Christ in prayer, we should do so in a spirit of quiet, heartfelt devotion to the One who gave His life so that we might have life eternal.

He was the Son of God, but He wore a crown of thorns. He was the Savior of mankind, yet He was put to death on a roughhewn cross made of wood. He offered His healing touch to an unsaved world, and yet the same hands that had healed the sick and raised the dead were pierced with nails.

Christ humbled Himself on a cross—for you. He shed His blood—for you. He has offered to walk with you through this life and throughout all eternity. As you approach Him today in prayer, think about His sacrifice and His grace. And be humble.

more stuff to think about

God is my heavenly Father. He loves me with
an everlasting love. The proof of that is the Cross.

ELISABETH ELLIOT

The cross takes care of the past.
The cross takes care of the flesh.
The cross takes care of the world.

KAY ARTHUR

Today's Prayer

Dear Jesus, You are my Savior and my protector. You suffered on the cross for me, and I will give You honor and praise every day of my life. I will honor You with my words, my thoughts, and my prayers. And I will live according to Your commandments, so that through me, others might come to know Your perfect love. Amen

for girls

Real Repentance

Come back to the LORD and live!
AMOS 5:6 NLT

Who among us has sinned? All of us. But, God calls upon us to turn away from sin by following His commandments. And the good news is this: When we do ask God's forgiveness and turn our hearts to Him, He forgives us absolutely and completely.

Genuine repentance requires more than simply offering God apologies for our misdeeds. Real repentance may start with feelings of sorrow and remorse, but it ends only when we turn away from the sin that has thus far distanced us from our Creator. In truth, we offer our most meaningful apologies to God, not with our words, but with our actions. As long as we are still engaged in sin, we may be "repenting," but we have not fully "repented."

Is there an aspect of your life that is distancing you from your God? If so, ask for His forgiveness, and—just as importantly—stop sinning. Then, wrap yourself in the protection of God's Word. When you do, you will be secure.

more stuff to think about

When true repentance comes, God will not hesitate for
a moment to forgive, cast the sins in the sea of forgetfulness,
and put the child on the road to restoration.

BETH MOORE

To do so no more is the truest repentance.

MARTIN LUTHER

Today's Prayer

When I stray from Your commandments, Lord, I must
not only confess my sins, I must also turn from them.
When I fall short, help me to change. When I reject Your
Word and Your will for my life, guide me back to Your
side. Forgive my sins, Dear Lord, and help me live
according to Your plan for my life. Your plan is perfect,
Father; I am not. Let me trust in You. Amen

for girls

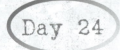

On Sad Days

Why am I so depressed? Why this turmoil within me?
Put your hope in God, for I will still praise Him,
my Savior and my God.

PSALM 42:11 HCSB

Some days are light and happy, and some days are not. When we face the inevitable dark days of life, we must choose how we will respond. Will we allow ourselves to sink even more deeply into our own sadness, or will we do the difficult work of pulling ourselves out? We bring light to the dark days of life by turning first to God, and then to trusted family members and friends. Then, we must go to work solving the problems that confront us. When we do, the clouds will eventually part, and the sun will shine once more upon our souls.

more stuff to think about

God is good, and heaven is forever.
These two facts should brighten up even the darkest day.

MARIE T. FREEMAN

When life is difficult, God wants us to have
a faith that trusts and waits.

KAY ARTHUR

Today's Prayer

Dear Heavenly Father, on those days when I am troubled, You comfort me if I turn my thoughts and prayers to You. When I am afraid, You protect me. When I am discouraged, You lift me up. You are my unending source of strength, Lord. In every circumstance, let me trust Your plan and Your will for my life. Amen

for girls

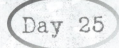

Day 25

God Is Love

*God is love, and the one who remains in love remains in
God, and God remains in him.*
1 John 4:16 HCSB

The Bible makes this promise: God is love. It's
a sweeping statement, a profoundly important
description of what God is and how God works. God's
love is perfect. When we open our hearts to His perfect
love, we are touched by the Creator's hand, and we are
transformed.

Today, even if you can only carve out a few quiet
moments, offer sincere prayers of thanksgiving to your
Creator. He loves you now and throughout all eternity. Open
your heart to His presence and His love.

2 minutes A DAY

more stuff to think about

I can tell you, from personal experience of walking with God
for over fifty years, that He is the Lover of my soul.

VONETTE BRIGHT

...God loves these people too, just because they're
unattractive or warped in their thinking doesn't mean
the Lord doesn't love them.

RUTH BELL GRAHAM

Today's Prayer

Dear Lord, the Bible tells me that You are my loving
Father. I thank You, Lord, for Your love and for Your
Son. Amen

for girls

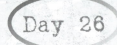

Obedience Now

*For God is working in you, giving you the desire to obey him
and the power to do what pleases him.*

PHILIPPIANS 2:13 NLT

God's commandments are not "suggestions," and they are not "helpful hints." They are, instead, immutable laws which, if followed, lead to repentance, salvation, and abundance. But if you choose to disobey the commandments of your Heavenly Father or the teachings of His Son, you will most surely reap a harvest of regret.

The formula for a successful life is surprisingly straightforward: Study God's Word and obey it. Does this sound too simple? Perhaps it is simple, but it is also the only way to reap the marvelous riches that God has in store for you.

more stuff to think about

God is God. Because He is God, He is worthy of my trust and obedience. I will find rest nowhere but in His holy will, a will that is unspeakably beyond my largest notions of what He is up to.

ELISABETH ELLIOT

The pathway of obedience can sometimes be difficult, but it always leads to a strengthening of our inner woman.

VONETTE BRIGHT

Today's Prayer

Dear Heavenly Father, You have blessed me with a love that is infinite and eternal. Let me demonstrate my love for You by obeying Your commandments. Make me a faithful servant, Father, today and throughout eternity. And, let me show my love for You by sharing Your message and Your love with others. Amen

for girls

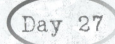

Day 27

Walking with the Wise

Listen to advice and accept correction,
and in the end you will be wise.
PROVERBS 19:20 NCV

D o you wish to become wise? Then you must walk with people who, by their words and their presence, make you wiser. And, to the best of your ability, you must avoid those people who encourage you to think foolish thoughts or do foolish things.

Today, as a gift to yourself, select, from your friends and family members, a mentor whose judgement you trust. Then, listen carefully to your mentor's advice and be willing to accept that advice, even if accepting it requires effort, or pain, or both. Consider your mentor to be God's gift to you. Thank God for that gift, and use it.

2 minutes a day

more stuff to think about

It takes a wise person to give good advice,
but an even wiser person to take it.

MARIE T. FREEMAN

The next best thing to being wise oneself is to live
in a circle of those who are.

C. S. LEWIS

Today's Prayer

Dear Lord, thank You for family members, for friends,
and for mentors. When I am troubled, let me turn
to them for help, for guidance, for comfort, and for
perspective. And Father, let me be a friend and mentor
to others, so that my love for You may be reflected in
my genuine concern for them. Amen

for girls

God First

Let us fix our eyes on Jesus, the author and perfecter of our faith, who for the joy set before him endured the cross, scorning its shame, and sat down at the right hand of the throne of God.

HEBREWS 12:2 NIV

Is God a big priority for you . . . or is He an afterthought? Do you give God your best or what's left? Have you given Christ your heart, your soul, your talents, your time, and your testimony? Or are you giving Him little more than a few hours each Sunday morning?

In the book of Exodus, God warns that we should place no gods before Him (Exodus 20:3). Yet all too often, we place our Lord in second, third, or fourth place as we worship the gods of pride, money, or personal gratification. When we unwittingly place possessions or relationships above our love for the Creator, we must realign our priorities or suffer the consequences.

Does God rule your heart? Make certain that the honest answer to this question is a resounding yes. In the life of every radical believer, God comes first. And that's precisely the place that He deserves in your heart.

more stuff to think about

The manifold rewards of a serious, consistent prayer life demonstrate clearly that time with our Lord should be our first priority.

SHIRLEY DOBSON

We set our eyes on the finish line, forgetting the past, and straining toward the mark of spiritual maturity and fruitfulness.

VONETTE BRIGHT

Today's Prayer

Lord, let Your priorities be my priorities. Let Your will be my will. Let Your Word be my guide, and let me grow in faith and in wisdom this day and every day. Amen

for girls

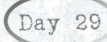

The Beauty of Humility

*For whoever exalts himself will be humbled,
and he who humbles himself will be exalted.*

LUKE 14:11 NKJV

Humility is not, in most cases, a naturally occurring human trait. Most of us, it seems, are more than willing to overestimate our own accomplishments. We are tempted to say, "Look how wonderful I am!" . . . hoping all the while that the world will agree with our own self-appraisals.

God honors humility . . . and He rewards those who humbly serve Him. When we acquire the wisdom to be humble, we bring enlightenment to the world (and blessings to ourselves).

But if we cannot overcome the tendency to overestimate our own accomplishments, then God still has some important lessons to teach us—lessons about the wisdom, the power, and the beauty of humility.

more stuff to think about

If you know who you are in Christ,
your personal ego is not an issue.

BETH MOORE

Humility is the fairest and rarest flower that blooms.

CHARLES SWINDOLL

Today's Prayer

Lord, You are great, and I am human. Keep me humble, and keep me mindful that all my gifts come from You. Amen

for girls

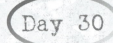

Discipline and Life

Discipline yourself for the purpose of godliness.

1 TIMOTHY 4:7 NASB

Are you a self-disciplined person? If so, congratulations . . . your disciplined approach to life can help you build a more meaningful relationship with God. Why? Because God expects all His believers (including you) to lead lives of disciplined obedience to Him . . . and He rewards those believers who do.

Sometimes, it's hard to be dignified and disciplined. Why? Because you live in a world where many prominent people want you to believe that dignified, self-disciplined behavior is going out of style. But don't kid yourself: self-discipline never goes out of style.

Face facts: Life's greatest rewards aren't likely to fall into your lap. To the contrary, your greatest accomplishments will probably require plenty of work and a heaping helping of self-discipline—which, by the way, is perfectly fine with God. After all, He knows that you're up to the task, and He has big plans for you. God will do His part to fulfill those plans, and the rest, of course, depends upon you.

more stuff to think about

Discipline is training that develops and corrects.

CHARLES STANLEY

The Bible calls for discipline and a recognition of authority. Children must learn this at home.

BILLY GRAHAM

Today's Prayer

Lord, I want to be a disciplined believer. Let me use my time wisely, and let me teach others by the faithfulness of my conduct, today and every day. Amen

for girls

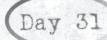

Courtesy According to God

Are there those among you who are truly wise and understanding? Then they should show it by living right and doing good things with a gentleness that comes from wisdom.

James 3:13 NCV

Does the Bible instruct us in matters of etiquette and courtesy? Of course it does. The words of Matthew 7:12 are clear: "In everything, therefore, treat people the same way you want them to treat you, for this is the Law and the Prophets" (NASB).

The Bible doesn't instruct, "In some things, treat people as you wish to be treated." And, it doesn't say, "From time to time, treat others with kindness." The Bible instructs us to treat others as we wish to be treated in every aspect of our daily lives.

Today try to be a little kinder than necessary to family members, friends, and total strangers. And as you consider all the things God has done for you, honor Him with your kind words and good deeds. He deserves no less, and neither do your loved ones.

more stuff to think about

Courtesy is contagious.

MARIE T. FREEMAN

Only the courteous can love,
but it is love that makes them courteous.

C. S. LEWIS

Today's Prayer

Guide me this day, O Lord, to treat all those I meet with courtesy and respect. You have created each person in Your own image; let me honor those who cross my path with the dignity that You have bestowed upon them. We are all Your children, Lord; let me show kindness to Your children. Amen

for girls

A Happy Christian

But happy are those . . . whose hope
is in the LORD their God.

Psalm 146:5 NLT

Happiness depends less upon our circumstances than upon our thoughts. When we turn our thoughts to God, to His gifts, and to His glorious creation, we experience the joy that God intends for His children. But, when we focus on the negative aspects of life, we suffer needlessly.

Do you sincerely want to be a happy Christian? Then set your mind and your heart upon God's love and His grace. The fullness of life in Christ is available to all who seek it and claim it. Count yourself among that number.

more stuff to think about

Christ is the secret, the source, the substance, the center, and the circumference of all true and lasting gladness.

MRS. CHARLES E. COWMAN

I am truly happy with Jesus Christ.
I couldn't live without Him.

Today's Prayer

Dear Lord, You are my strength and my joy. I will rejoice in the day that You have made, and I will give thanks for the countless blessings that You have given me. Let me be a joyful Christian, Father, as I share the Good News of Your Son, and let me praise You for all the marvelous things You have done. Amen

for girls

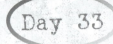

No More Gossip!

Though some tongues just love the taste of gossip,
Christians have better uses for language than that.
Don't talk dirty or silly. That kind of talk doesn't fit our style.
Thanksgiving is our dialect.

EPHESIANS 5:4 MSG

Face it: gossip is bad—and the Bible clearly tells us that gossip is wrong.

When we say things that we don't want other people to know we said, we're being somewhat dishonest, but if the things we say aren't true, we're being very dishonest. Either way, we have done something that we may regret later, especially when the other person finds out.

So do yourself a big favor: don't gossip. It's a waste of words, and it's the wrong thing to do. You'll feel better about yourself if you don't gossip (and other people will feel better about you, too). So don't do it!

more stuff to think about

To belittle is to be little.

Change the heart, and you change the speech.

WARREN WIERSBE

Today's Prayer

Dear Lord, You hear every word that I say. Let my speech bring honor to You and to Your Son. Today and every day, let me speak words that are honest, kind, and worthy of You. Amen

for girls

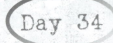

Who Will You Follow?

*If anyone would come after me, he must deny himself
and take up his cross and follow me.*

MARK 8:34 NIV

There's really no way around it: If you want to know God, you've got to get to know His Son. And that's good, because getting to know Jesus can—and should—be the most enriching experience of your life.

Jesus doesn't want you to be a lukewarm believer; Jesus wants you to be a "new creation" through Him. And that's exactly what you should want for yourself, too. Nothing is more important than your wholehearted commitment to your Creator and to His only begotten Son. Your faith must never be an afterthought; it must be your ultimate priority, your ultimate possession, and your ultimate passion.

You are the recipient of Christ's love. Accept it enthusiastically and share it passionately. Jesus deserves your undivided attention. And when you give it to Him, you'll be forever grateful that you did.

more stuff to think about

I can tell you, from personal experience of walking with God
for over fifty years, that He is the Lover of my soul.

VONETTE BRIGHT

It's your heart that Jesus longs for: your will to be made
His own with self on the cross forever,
and Jesus alone on the throne.

RUTH BELL GRAHAM

Today's Prayer

Dear Jesus, because I am Your disciple, I will trust
You, I will obey Your teachings, and I will share Your
Good News. You have given me life abundant and life
eternal, and I will follow You today and forever. Amen

for girls

Encouraging Others

*Let's see how inventive we can be in encouraging love
and helping out, not avoiding worshipping together
as some do but spurring each other on.*
HEBREWS 10:24-25 MSG

One of the reasons that God placed you here on earth is so that you might become a beacon of encouragement to the world. As a faithful follower of the One from Galilee, you have every reason to be hopeful, and you have every reason to share your hopes with others. When you do, you will discover that hope, like other human emotions, is contagious.

As a follower of Christ, you are instructed to choose your words carefully so as to build others up through wholesome, honest encouragement (Ephesians 4:29). So look for the good in others and celebrate the good that you find. As the old saying goes, "When someone does something good, applaud—you'll make two people happy."

more stuff to think about

Encouraging others means helping people,
looking for the best in them, and trying to
bring out their positive qualities.

JOHN MAXWELL

As you're rushing through life, take time to stop a moment,
look into people's eyes, say something kind,
and try to make them laugh!

BARBARA JOHNSON

Today's Prayer

Dear Lord, let me celebrate the accomplishments
of others. Make me a source of genuine, lasting
encouragement to my family and friends. And let my
words and deeds be worthy of Your Son, the One who
gives me strength and salvation, this day and for all
eternity. Amen

for girls

God's Promises

Patient endurance is what you need now,
so you will continue to do God's will. Then you will receive
all that he has promised.

HEBREWS 10:36 NLT

God has made quite a few promises to you, and He intends to keep every single one of them. You will find these promises in a book like no other: the Holy Bible. The Bible is your roadmap for life here on earth and for life eternal. As a believer, you are called upon to trust its promises, to follow its commandments, and to share its Good News.

God has made promises to all of humanity and to you. God's promises never fail and they never grow old. You must trust those promises and share them with your family, with your friends, and with the world . . . starting now . . . and ending never.

more stuff to think about

Shake the dust from your past, and move forward
in His promises.

KAY ARTHUR

Claim all of God's promises in the Bible. Your sins,
your worries, your life—you may cast them all on Him.

CORRIE TEN BOOM

Today's Prayer

Lord, Your Holy Word contains promises, and I will
trust them. I will use the Bible as my guide, and I will
trust You, Lord, to speak to me through Your Holy
Spirit and through Your Holy Word, this day and
forever. Amen

Too Many Distractions?

Keep your eyes on Jesus, who both began and finished this race we're in. Study how he did it. Because he never lost sight of where he was headed, that exhilarating finish in and with God, he could put up with anything along the way: cross, shame, whatever. And now he's there, in the place of honor, right alongside God.

HEBREWS 12:2 MSG

All of us must live through those days when the traffic jams, the computer crashes, and the dog makes a main course out of our homework. But, when we find ourselves distracted by the minor frustrations of life, we must catch ourselves, take a deep breath, and lift our thoughts upward.

Although we may, at times, struggle mightily to rise above the distractions of everyday living, we need never struggle alone. God is here—eternal and faithful, with infinite patience and love—and, if we reach out to Him, He will restore our sense of perspective and give peace to our souls.

more stuff to think about

When Jesus is in our midst, He brings His limitless power
along as well. But, Jesus must be in the middle,
all eyes and hearts focused on Him.

SHIRLEY DOBSON

We need to stop focusing on our lacks and stop giving out
excuses and start looking at and listening to Jesus.

ANNE GRAHAM LOTZ

Today's Prayer

Dear Lord, help me to face this day with a spirit of
optimism and thanksgiving. And let me focus my
thoughts on You and Your incomparable gifts. Amen

for girls

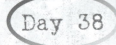

Too Impulsive?

Enthusiasm without knowledge is not good.
If you act too quickly, you might make a mistake.
PROVERBS 19:2 NCV

A re you, at times, just a little bit impulsive? Do you occasionally leap before you look? Do you react first and think about your reaction second? If so, God wants to have a little chat with you.

God's Word is clear: as believers, we are called to lead lives of discipline, diligence, moderation, and maturity. But the world often tempts us to behave otherwise. Everywhere we turn, or so it seems, we are faced with powerful temptations to behave in undisciplined, ungodly ways.

God's Word instructs us to be disciplined in our thoughts and our actions; God's Word warns us against the dangers of impulsive behavior. God's Word teaches us that "anger" is only one letter away from "danger." And, as believers in a just God who means what He says, we should act—and react—accordingly.

more stuff to think about

Waiting on God brings us to the journey's end
quicker than our feet.

MRS. CHARLES E. COWMAN

God never hurries. There are no deadlines against which
He must work. To know this is to quiet our spirits
and relax our nerves.

A. W. TOZER

Today's Prayer

Lord, sometimes I can be an impulsive person. Slow me
down, calm me down, and help me make wise decisions
. . . today and every day of my life. Amen

for girls

God's Abundance

I came that they may have life, and have it abundantly.
JOHN 10:10 NASB

Are you the kind of young woman who accepts God's spiritual abundance without reservation? If so, you are availing yourself of the peace and the joy that He has promised. Do you sincerely seek the riches that our Savior offers to those who give themselves to Him? Then follow Him. When you do, you will receive the love and the abundance that Jesus offers to those who follow Him.

Seek first the salvation that is available through a personal, passionate relationship with Christ, and then claim the joy, the peace, and the spiritual abundance that the Shepherd offers His sheep.

more stuff to think about

Jesus intended for us to be overwhelmed by the blessings of regular days. He said it was the reason he had come: "I am come that they might have life, and that they might have it more abundantly."

GLORIA GAITHER

If we were given all we wanted here, our hearts would settle for this world rather than the next.

ELISABETH ELLIOT

Today's Prayer

Dear Lord, You have offered me the gift of abundance through Your Son. Thank You, Father, for the abundant life that is mine through Christ Jesus. Let me accept His gifts and use them always to glorify You. Amen

for girls

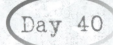

The Search for Purpose

The lines of purpose in your lives never grow slack,
tightly tied as they are to your future in heaven,
kept taut by hope.
COLOSSIANS 1:5 MSG

"What on earth does God intend for me to do with my life?" It's an easy question to ask but, for many of us, a difficult question to answer. Why? Because God's purposes aren't always clear to us. Sometimes, we wander aimlessly in a wilderness of our own making. And sometimes, we struggle mightily against God in an unsuccessful attempt to find success and happiness through our own means, not His.

Are you genuinely trying to figure out God's purpose for your life? If so, you can be sure that with God's help, you will eventually discover it. So keep praying, and keep watching. And rest assured: God's got big plans for you . . . very big plans.

more stuff to think about

Each one of us is God's special work of art. Through us, He teaches and inspires, delights and encourages, informs and uplifts all those who view our lives. God, the master artist, is most concerned about expressing Himself—His thoughts and His intentions—through what He paints in our character.... [He] wants to paint a beautiful portrait of His Son in and through your life.
A painting like no other in all of time.

JONI EARECKSON TADA

Today's Prayer

Lord, You've got something You want me to do—help me to figure out exactly what it is. Give me Your blessings and lead me along a path that is pleasing to You . . . today, tomorrow, and forever. Amen

for girls

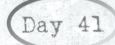

A Willingness to Serve

Whoever wants to become great among you must serve the rest of you like a servant.

MATTHEW 20:26 NCV

The words of Jesus are clear: the most esteemed men and women in this world are not the big-shots who jump up on stage and hog the spotlight; the greatest among us are those who are willing to become humble servants.

Today, you may be tempted to take more than you give. But if you feel the urge to be selfish, resist that urge with all your might. Don't be stingy, selfish, or self-absorbed. Instead, serve your friends quietly and without fanfare. Find a need and fill it . . . humbly. Lend a helping hand...anonymously. Share a word of kindness . . . with quiet sincerity. As you go about your daily activities, remember that the Savior of all humanity made Himself a servant, and we, as His followers, must do no less.

more stuff to think about

God wants us to serve Him with a willing spirit,
one that would choose no other way.

BETH MOORE

Christianity, in its purest form, is nothing more than seeing
Jesus. Christian service, in its purest form, is nothing more
than imitating Him who we see. To see His Majesty and
to imitate Him: that is the sum of Christianity.

MAX LUCADO

Today's Prayer

Dear Lord, help me to make Your world a better place.
I can't fix all the world's troubles, but I can help make
things better with kind words, good deeds, and sincere
prayers. Let my actions and my prayers be pleasing to
You, Lord, now and forever. Amen

for girls

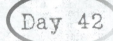

God's Good News

Thanks be to God for his indescribable gift!
2 CORINTHIANS 9:15 NIV

Here's the great news: God's grace is not earned . . . and thank goodness it's not! If God's grace were some sort of reward for good behavior, none of us could earn enough brownie points to win the big prize. But it doesn't work that way. Grace is a free offer from God. By accepting that offer, we transform our lives today and forever.

God's grace is not just any old gift; it's the ultimate gift, and we owe Him our eternal gratitude. Our Heavenly Father is waiting patiently for each of us to accept His Son and receive His grace. Let us accept that gift today so that we might enjoy God's presence now and throughout all eternity.

God does amazing works through prayers
that seek to extend His grace to others.

SHIRLEY DOBSON

No one is beyond His grace. No situation,
anywhere on earth, it too hard for God.

JIM CYMBALA

Today's Prayer

Accepting Your grace can be hard, Lord. Somehow, I
feel that I must earn Your love and Your acceptance.
Yet, the Bible promises that You love me and save me
by Your grace. It is a gift I can only accept and cannot
earn. Thank You for Your priceless, everlasting gift.
Amen

for girls

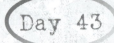

Excuses Everywhere

Each of us will be rewarded for his own hard work.
1 CORINTHIANS 3:8 TLB

Excuses are everywhere . . . excellence is not. Whether you're a student or a corporate CEO, your work is a picture book of your priorities. So whatever your job description, it's up to you, and no one else, to become masterful at your craft. It's up to you to do your job right, and to do it right now.

Because we humans are such creative excuse-makers, all of the best excuses have already been taken—we've heard them all before.

So if you're wasting your time trying to concoct a new and improved excuse, don't bother. It's impossible. A far better strategy is this: do the work. Now. Then, let your excellent work speak loudly and convincingly for itself.

more stuff to think about

Replace your excuses with fresh determination.

An excuse is only the skin of a reason stuffed with a lie.

VANCE HAVNER

Today's Prayer

Heavenly Father, how easy it is to make excuses. But, I want to be a girl who accomplishes important work for You. Help me, Father, to strive for excellence, not excuses. Amen

for girls

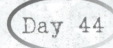

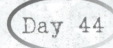 Day 44

Not in Denial

We justify our actions by appearances;
God examines our motives.

PROVERBS 21:2 MSG

If we deny our sins, we allow those sins to flourish. And if we allow sinful behaviors to become habits, we invite hardships into our own lives and into the lives of our loved ones. When we yield to the distractions and temptations of this troubled world, we suffer. But God has other intentions, and His plans for our lives do not include sin or denial.

When we allow ourselves to encounter God's presence, He will lead us away from temptation, away from confusion, and away from the self-deception. God is the champion of truth and the enemy of denial. May we see ourselves through His eyes and conduct ourselves accordingly.

2 MINUTES A DAY

more stuff to think about

The single most important element in any human relationship is honesty—with oneself, with God, and with others.

CATHERINE MARSHALL

What I like about experience is that it is such an honest thing. You may take any number of wrong turnings; but keep your eyes open and you will not be allowed to go very far before the warning signs appear. You may have deceived yourself, but experience is not trying to deceive you. The universe rings true wherever you fairly test it.

C. S. LEWIS

Today's Prayer

Dear Lord, help me see the truth, and help me respond to the things that I see with determination, wisdom, and courage. Amen

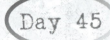

Day 45

The Ultimate Protection

My God is my rock, in whom I take refuge,
my shield and the horn of my salvation.
2 Samuel 22:2-3 NIV

God has promised to protect us, and He intends to keep His promise. In a world filled with dangers and temptations, God is the ultimate armor. In a world filled with misleading messages, God's Word is the ultimate truth. In a world filled with more frustrations than we can count, God's Son offers the ultimate peace.

Will you accept God's peace and wear God's armor against the dangers of our world? Hopefully so—because when you do, you can live courageously, knowing that you possess the ultimate protection: God's unfailing love for you.

more stuff to think about

Prayer is our pathway not only to divine protection, but also to a personal, intimate relationship with God.

SHIRLEY DOBSON

The Will of God will never take you where the Grace of God will not protect you.

ANONYMOUS

Today's Prayer

Lord, You have promised to protect me, and I will trust You. Today, I will live courageously as I place my hopes, my faith, and life in Your hands. Let my life be a testimony to the transforming power of Your love, Your Grace, and Your Son. Amen

for girls

The Right Kind of Fear

The fear of the Lord is the beginning of knowledge,
but fools despise wisdom and discipline.

PROVERBS 1:7 NIV

Are you a young woman who possesses a healthy, fearful respect for God's power? Hopefully so. After all, God's Word teaches that the fear of the Lord is the beginning of knowledge (Proverbs 1:7).

When we fear the Creator—and when we honor Him by obeying His commandments—we receive God's approval and His blessings. But, when we ignore Him or disobey His commandments, we invite disastrous consequences.

God's hand shapes the universe, and it shapes our lives. God maintains absolute sovereignty over His creation, and His power is beyond comprehension. The fear of the Lord is, indeed, the beginning of knowledge. But thankfully, once we possess a healthy, reverent fear of God, we need never be fearful of anything else.

more stuff to think about

The remarkable thing about fearing God is that when you
fear God, you fear nothing else, whereas if you
do not fear God, you fear everything else.

OSWALD CHAMBERS

The fear of God is the death of every other fear.

C. H. SPURGEON

Today's Prayer

Dear Lord, others have expectations of me, and I have
hopes and desires for my life. Lord, bring all other
expectations in line with Your plans for me. May my
only fear be that of displeasing the One who created me.
May I obey Your commandments and seek Your will
this day and every day. Amen

for girls

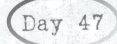

Critics Beware

Don't speak evil against each other, my dear brothers and sisters. If you criticize each other and condemn each other, then you are criticizing and condemning God's law. But you are not a judge who can decide whether the law is right or wrong. Your job is to obey it.

JAMES 4:11 NLT

From experience, we know that it is easier to criticize than to correct. And we know that it is easier to find faults than solutions. Yet the urge to criticize others remains a powerful temptation for most of us. Our task, as obedient believers, is to break the twin habits of negative thinking and critical speech.

Negativity is highly contagious: we give it to others who, in turn, give it back to us. This cycle can be broken by positive thoughts, heartfelt prayers, and encouraging words. As thoughtful servants of a loving God, we can use the transforming power of Christ's love to break the chains of negativity. And we should.

more stuff to think about

Judging draws the judgment of others.

CATHERINE MARSHALL

Being critical of others, including God,
is one way we try to avoid facing
and judging our own sins.

WARREN WIERSBE

Today's Prayer

Help me, Lord, rise above the need to criticize others.
May my own shortcomings humble me, and may I
always be a source of genuine encouragement to my
family and friends. Amen

for girls

Big Dreams

*Live full lives, full in the fullness of God. God can do
anything, you know—far more than you could ever imagine
or guess or request in your wildest dreams!
He does it not by pushing us around but by working
within us, his Spirit deeply and gently within us.*

EPHESIANS 3:19-20 MSG

Are you willing to entertain the possibility that God
has big plans in store for you? Hopefully so. Yet
sometimes, especially if you've recently experienced
a life-altering disappointment, you may find it difficult to
envision a brighter future for yourself and your family. If so,
it's time to reconsider your own capabilities . . . and God's.

Your heavenly Father created you with unique gifts and
untapped talents; your job is to tap them. When you do,
you'll begin to feel an increasing sense of confidence in
yourself and in your future.

It takes courage to dream big dreams. You will discover
that courage when you do three things: accept the past, trust
God to handle the future, and make the most of the time He
has given you today.

Nothing is too difficult for God, and no dreams are
too big for Him—not even yours. So start living—and
dreaming—accordingly.

You cannot out-dream God.

JOHN ELDREDGE

Allow your dreams a place in your prayers and plans.
God-given dreams can help you move into
the future He is preparing for you.

BARBARA JOHNSON

Today's Prayer

Dear Lord, give me the courage to dream and the
faithfulness to trust in Your perfect plan. When I am
worried or weary, give me strength for today and hope
for tomorrow. Keep me mindful of Your healing power,
Your infinite love, and Your eternal salvation. Amen

Your Testimony

And I assure you of this: If anyone acknowledges me publicly here on earth, I, the Son of Man, will openly acknowledge that person in the presence of God's angels. But if anyone denies me here on earth, I will deny that person before God's angels.

LUKE 12:8-9 NLT

Let's face facts: those of us who are Christians should be willing to talk about the things that Christ has done for us. Our personal testimonies are vitally important, but sometimes, because of shyness or insecurities, we're afraid to share our experiences. And that's unfortunate.

We live in a world that desperately needs the healing message of Christ Jesus. Every believer, each in his or her own way, bears responsibility for sharing the Good News of our Savior. And it is important to remember that we bear testimony through both words and actions.

If you seek to be a radical follower of Christ, then it's time for you to share your testimony with others. So today, preach the Gospel through your words and your deeds…but not necessarily in that order.

more stuff to think about

There is nothing anybody else can do that can stop God from using us. We can turn everything into a testimony.

CORRIE TEN BOOM

Claim the joy that is yours. Pray.
And know that your joy is used by God to reach others.

KAY ARTHUR

Today's Prayer

Lord, the life that I live and the words that I speak will tell the world how I feel about You. Today and every day, let my testimony be worthy of You. Let my words be sure and true, and let my actions point others to You. Amen

for girls

Today's Decisions

The righteous will live by his faith.

HABAKKUK 2:4 NIV

Everyday life is an adventure in decision-making. Each day, we make countless decisions that hopefully bring us closer to God. When we obey God's commandments, we share in His abundance and His peace. But, when we turn our backs upon God by disobeying Him, we invite Old Man Trouble to stop by for an extended visit.

Do you want to be successful and happy? If so, here's a good place to start: Obey God. When you're faced with a difficult choice or a powerful temptation, pray about it. Invite God into your heart and live according to His commandments. When you do, you will be blessed today, tomorrow, and forever.

more stuff to think about

Righteousness comes only from God.

KAY ARTHUR

Holiness is not an impossibility for any of us.

ELISABETH ELLIOT

Today's Prayer

Lord, Your laws are perfect; let me live by those laws. And, let my life be a testimony to the power of righteousness and to the wisdom of Your commandments. Amen

for girls

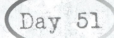

Your Wonderful Life

I have set before you life and death, blessings and curses.
Now choose life, so that you and your children may live
and that you may love the LORD your God,
listen to his voice, and hold fast to him.

DEUTERONOMY 30:19-20 NIV

Life can be tough sometimes, but it's also wonderful—and it's a glorious gift from God. Every day, including this one, comes gift-wrapped from God—your job is to unwrap that gift, to use it wisely, and to give thanks to the Giver.

Instead of sleepwalking through life, you must wake up and live in the precious present. Each waking moment holds the potential to celebrate, to serve, to share, or to love. Because you are a person with incalculable potential, each moment has incalculable value. Your challenge is to experience each day to the full as you seek to live in accordance with God's plan for your life. When you do, you'll experience His abundance and His peace.

Are you willing to treat this day (and every one hereafter) as a special gift to be savored and celebrated? You should—and if you seek to Live with a capital L, you most certainly will.

more stuff to think about

The Christian life is motivated, not by a list of do's
and don'ts, but by the gracious outpouring
of God's love and blessing.

ANNE GRAHAM LOTZ

Life is a glorious opportunity.

BILLY GRAHAM

Today's Prayer

Lord, You have given me the gift of life. Let me treasure
it, and let me use it for Your service and for Your glory.
Amen

for girls

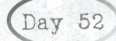

How Much Love?

*We know how much God loves us, and we have put
our trust in him. God is love, and all who live in love
live in God, and God lives in them.*

1 JOHN 4:16 NLT

How much does God love you? As long as you're alive, you'll never be able to figure it out because God's love is just too big to comprehend. But this much we know: God loves you so much that He sent His Son Jesus to come to this earth and to die for you! And, when you accepted Jesus into your heart, God gave you a gift that is more precious than gold: the gift of eternal life.

God's love is bigger and more powerful than anybody can imagine, but His love is very real. So do yourself a favor right now: accept God's love with open arms and welcome His Son, Jesus, into your heart. When you do, your life will be changed today, tomorrow, and forever.

more stuff to think about

Jesus loves us with fidelity, purity, constancy,
and passion, no matter how imperfect we are.

STORMIE OMARTIAN

Nails didn't hold Jesus on the cross. His love for you did.

ANONYMOUS

Today's Prayer

Dear Lord, the Bible tells me that You are my loving
Father. I thank You, Lord, for Your love and for Your
Son. Amen

for girls

The Book God Wrote

*For I am not ashamed of the gospel of Christ, for it is the
power of God to salvation for everyone who believes.*

Romans 1:16 NKJV

As you establish priorities for life, you must decide
whether God's Word will be a bright spotlight that
guides your path every day or a tiny nightlight that
occasionally flickers in the dark. The decision to study the
Bible—or not—is yours and yours alone. But make no
mistake: how you choose to use your Bible will have a
profound impact on you and your loved ones.

The Bible is unlike any other book. It is a priceless gift
from your Creator, a tool that God intends for you to use
in every aspect of you life. And, it contains promises upon
which you, as a Christian, can and must depend.

Jonathan Edwards advised, "Be assiduous in reading the
Holy Scriptures. This is the fountain whence all knowledge in
divinity must be derived. Therefore let not this treasure lie by
you neglected."

God's Holy Word is, indeed, a priceless, one-of-a-kind
treasure. Handle it with care, but more importantly, handle it
every day.

more stuff to think about

Study the Bible and observe how the persons behaved and how God dealt with them. There is explicit teaching on every condition of life.

CORRIE TEN BOOM

The reference point for the Christian is the Bible. All values, judgments, and attitudes must be gauged in relationship to this reference point.

RUTH BELL GRAHAM

Today's Prayer

Dear Lord, the Bible is Your gift to me. Let me use it, let me trust it, and let me obey it, today and every day that I live. Amen

for girls

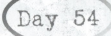

What Kind of Example?

Be an example to the believers in word, in conduct,
in love, in spirit, in faith, in purity.
1 TIMOTHY 4:12 NKJV

How do people know that you're a Christian? Well, you can tell them, of course. And make no mistake about it: talking about your faith in God is a very good thing to do. But simply telling people about Jesus isn't enough. You must also be willing to show people how a radical Christian (like you) should behave.

Jesus never comes "next." He is always first. And, if you seek to follow Him, you must do so every day of the week, not just on Sundays. After all, you are indeed "the light that gives light to the world," and shouldn't your light shine all the time? Of course it should. God deserves no less, and neither, for that matter, do you.

more stuff to think about

Living life with a consistent spiritual walk deeply influences those we love most.

VONETTE BRIGHT

In your desire to share the gospel, you may be the only Jesus someone else will ever meet. Be real and be involved with people.

BARBARA JOHNSON

Today's Prayer

Lord, make me a worthy example to my family and friends. And, let my words and my deeds serve as a testimony to the changes You have made in my life. Let me praise You, Father, by following in the footsteps of Your Son, and let others see Him through me. Amen

for girls

Very Big Plans

Teach me to do Your will, for You are my God. May Your gracious Spirit lead me on level ground.
PSALM 143:10 HCSB

The Bible makes it clear: God's got a plan—a very big plan—and you're an important part of that plan. But here's the catch: God won't force His plans upon you; you've got to figure things out for yourself . . . or not.

As a follower of Christ, you should ask yourself this question: "How closely can I make my plans match God's plans?" The more closely you manage to follow the path that God intends for your life, the better.

Do you have questions or concerns about the future? Take them to God in prayer. Do you have hopes and expectations? Talk to God about your dreams. Are you carefully planning for the days and weeks ahead? Consult God as you establish your priorities. Turn every concern over to your Heavenly Father, and sincerely seek His guidance—prayerfully, earnestly, and often. Then, listen for His answers . . . and trust the answers that He gives.

more stuff to think about

God prepared a plan for your life alone—and neither man nor the devil can destroy that plan.

KAY ARTHUR

We will stand amazed to see the topside of the tapestry and how God beautifully embroidered each circumstance into a pattern for our good and His glory.

JONI EARECKSON TADA

Today's Prayer

Lord, You have a plan for my life that is grander than I can imagine. Let Your purposes be my purposes. Let Your will be my will. When I am confused, give me clarity. When I am frightened, give me courage. Let me be Your faithful servant, always seeking Your guidance for my life. And, let me always be a shining beacon for Your Son today, and every day that I live. Amen

for girls

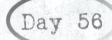
A Rule That's Golden

Do to others as you would have them do to you.
LUKE 6:31 NIV

Would you like to make the world a better place? If so, you can start by being a girlfriend who practices the Golden Rule.

Some rules are easier to understand than they are to live by, and the Golden Rule certainly fits that description. Jesus told us that we should treat other people in the same way that we would want to be treated. But sometimes, especially when we're tired, upset, jealous, or insecure, that rule is very hard to follow.

Jesus wants us to treat other people with respect, kindness, courtesy, and love. When we do, we make our families and friends happy . . . and we make our Father in heaven very proud.

So if you're wondering how to make the world a better place, here's a great place to start: let the Golden Rule be your rule, too. And if you want to know how to treat other people, ask the girl you see every time you look into the mirror. The answer you receive from her will tell you exactly what to do.

more stuff to think about

The Golden Rule starts at home,
but it should never stop there.

MARIE T. FREEMAN

I have discovered that when I please Christ,
I end up inadvertently serving others far more effectively.

BETH MOORE

Today's Prayer

Lord, in all aspects of my life, let me treat others as I wish to be treated. The Golden Rule is Your rule, Father; let me make it mine. Amen

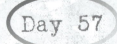

Behaving Differently

So don't get tired of doing what is good.
Don't get discouraged and give up, for we will reap
a harvest of blessing at the appropriate time.

GALATIANS 6:9 NLT

Okay, girlfriend, answer this question honestly: Do you behave differently because of your relationship with Jesus? Or do you behave in pretty much the same way that you would if you weren't a believer? Hopefully, the fact that you've invited Christ to reign over your heart means that you've made BIG changes in your thoughts and your actions.

Doing the right thing is not always easy, especially when you're tired or frustrated. But, doing the wrong thing almost always leads to trouble. And sometimes, it leads to big trouble.

If you're determined to follow "the crowd," you may soon find yourself headed in the wrong direction. So here's some advice: Don't follow the crowd—follow Jesus. And keep following Him every day of your life.

more stuff to think about

Either God's Word keeps you from sin,
or sin keeps you from God's Word.

Corrie ten Boom

There may be no trumpet sound or loud applause
when we make a right decision, just a calm sense
of resolution and peace.

Gloria Gaither

Today's Prayer

Lord, there is a right way and a wrong way to live. Let
me live according to Your rules, not the world's rules.
Your path is right for me, God; let me follow it every
day of my life. Amen

for girls

Love According to God

But now abide faith, hope, love, these three;
but the greatest of these is love.

1 CORINTHIANS 13:13 NASB

Love, like everything else in this wonderful world, begins and ends with God, but the middle part belongs to us. During the brief time that we have here on earth, God has given each of us the opportunity to become a loving person—or not. God has given each of us the opportunity to be kind, to be courteous, to be cooperative, and to be forgiving—or not.

The Christian path is an exercise in love and forgiveness. If you are to walk in Christ's footsteps, you must forgive those who have done you harm, and you must accept Christ's love by sharing it freely with family, friends, neighbors, and even strangers.

Building lasting relationships requires compassion, wisdom, empathy, kindness, courtesy, and forgiveness. If that sounds a lot like work, it is—which is perfectly fine with God. Why? Because He knows that you are capable of doing that work, and because He knows that the fruits of your labors will enrich the lives of your loved ones and the lives of generations yet unborn.

more stuff to think about

It is when we come to the Lord in our nothingness,
our powerlessness and our helplessness that He then
enables us to love in a way which, without Him,
would be absolutely impossible.

ELISABETH ELLIOT

Those who abandon ship the first time it enters a storm miss
the calm beyond. And the rougher the storms weathered
together, the deeper and stronger real love grows.

RUTH BELL GRAHAM

Today's Prayer

Dear Lord, today and every day, I will tell my family
that I love them. And I will show my family that I love
them, too. Amen

for girls

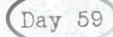

Media Messages

Set your mind on the things above,
not on the things that are on earth.

COLOSSIANS 3:2 NASB

Sometimes it's hard being a Christian, especially when the world keeps pumping out messages that are contrary to your faith.

The media is working around the clock in an attempt to rearrange your priorities. The media says that your appearance is all-important, that your clothes are all-important, that your relationships with guys are all-important, and that partying is all-important. But guess what? Those messages are lies. The "all-important" things in your life have little to do with parties and appearances. The all-important things in life have to do with your faith, your family, and your future. Period.

Are you willing to stand up for your faith? Are you willing to stand up and be counted, not just in church, where it's relatively easy to be a Christian, but also out there in the "real" world, where it's hard? Hopefully so, because you owe it to God and you owe it to yourself.

more stuff to think about

The more we stuff ourselves with material pleasures,
the less we seem to appreciate life.

BARBARA JOHNSON

Our fight is not against any physical enemy;
it is against organizations and powers that are spiritual.
We must struggle against sin all our lives,
but we are assured we will win.

CORRIE TEN BOOM

Today's Prayer

Lord, this world is a crazy place, and I have many
opportunities to stray from Your commandments. Help
me turn to obey You! Let me keep Christ in my heart,
and let me put the devil in his place: far away from me!
Amen

for girls

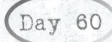

Making Time to Praise God

*So through Jesus let us always offer to God our sacrifice
of praise, coming from lips that speak his name.*
HEBREWS 13:15 NCV

Your life is probably hectic, demanding, and complicated. And when the demands of life leave you rushing from place to place with scarcely a moment to spare, you may not take time to praise your Creator. Big mistake.

The Bible makes it clear: it pays to praise God. Worship and praise should be a part of everything you do. Otherwise, you quickly lose perspective as you fall prey to the demands of everyday life.

Do you sincerely desire to know God in a more meaningful way? Then praise Him for who He is and for what He has done for you. And please don't wait until Sunday morning—praise Him all day long, every day, for as long as you live . . . and then for all eternity.

more stuff to think about

Nothing we do is more powerful or
more life-changing than praising God.

STORMIE OMARTIAN

Two wings are necessary to lift our souls toward God:
prayer and praise. Prayer asks.
Praise accepts the answer.

MRS. CHARLES E. COWMAN

Today's Prayer

Dear Lord, today and every day we will praise You. We
will come to You with hope in our hearts and words of
gratitude on our lips. Let our thoughts, our prayers, our
words, and our deeds praise You now and forever. Amen

for girls

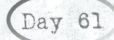
Day 61

Every Day with God

Stay clear of silly stories that get dressed up as religion.
Exercise daily in God—no spiritual flabbiness, please!
1 TIMOTHY 4:7 MSG

Daily life is a tapestry of habits, and no habit is more important to your spiritual health than the discipline of daily prayer and devotion to the Creator. When you begin each day with your head bowed and your heart lifted, you are reminded of God's love and God's laws.

Each day has 1,440 minutes—do you value your relationship with God enough to spend a few of those minutes with Him? He deserves that much of your time and more. But if you find that you're simply "too busy" for a daily chat with your Father in heaven, it's time to take a long, hard look at your priorities and your values.

If you've acquired the unfortunate habit of trying to "squeeze" God into the corners of your life, it's time to reshuffle the items on your to-do list by placing God first. God wants your undivided attention, not the leftovers of your day. So, if you haven't already done so, form the habit of spending quality time with your Creator. He deserves it . . . and so, for that matter, do you.

more stuff to think about

God is a place of safety you can run to,
but it helps if you are running to Him on a daily basis
so that you are in familiar territory.

STORMIE OMARTIAN

If you, too, will learn to wait upon God, to get alone
with Him, and remain silent so that you can hear
His voice when He is ready to speak to you,
what a difference it will make in you life!

KAY ARTHUR

Today's Prayer

Dear Lord, help me to hear Your direction for my life in
the solitary moments that I spend with You. And as I
fulfill my responsibilities throughout the day, let my
actions and my thoughts be pleasing to You. Amen

for girls

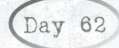

He Answers

If you believe, you will receive whatever you ask for in prayer.

MATTHEW 21:22 NIV

In case you've been wondering, wonder no more—God does answer your prayers. What God does not do is this: He does not always answer your prayers as soon as you might like, and He does not always answer your prayers by saying "Yes."

God isn't an order-taker, and He's not some sort of cosmic vending machine. Sometimes—even when we want something very badly—our loving Heavenly Father responds to our requests by saying "No", and we must accept His answer, even if we don't understand it.

God answers prayers not only according to our wishes but also according to His master plan. We cannot know that plan, but we can know the Planner . . . and we must trust His wisdom, His righteousness, and His love.

Of this you can be sure: God is listening, and He wants to hear from you now. So what are you waiting for?

more stuff to think about

As we join together in prayer, we draw on
God's enabling might in a way that multiplies
our own efforts many times over.

SHIRLEY DOBSON

When you ask God to do something, don't ask timidly;
put your whole heart into it.

MARIE T. FREEMAN

Today's Prayer

Lord, make me a prayerful Christian. In good times
and in bad times, in whatever state I find myself,
let me turn my prayers to You. You always hear my
prayers, God; let me always pray them! Amen

for girls

The Best Time to Celebrate

Celebrate God all day, every day. I mean, revel in him!
PHILIPPIANS 4:4 MSG

What is the best day to celebrate life? This one! Today and every day should be a time for celebration as we consider the Good News of God's gift: salvation through Jesus Christ.

What do you expect from the day ahead? Are you expecting God to do wonderful things, or are you living beneath a cloud of worry and doubt?

The familiar words of Psalm 118:24 remind us of a profound yet simple truth: "This is the day which the LORD has made." Our duty, as believers, is to rejoice in God's marvelous creation. For Christians, every day begins and ends with God and His Son. Christ came to this earth to give us abundant life and eternal salvation. We give thanks to our Maker when we treasure each day. So with no further ado, let the celebration begin!

2 minutes A DAY

more stuff to think about

If you can forgive the person you were, accept the person you are, and believe in the person you will become, you are headed for joy. So celebrate your life.

BARBARA JOHNSON

Unparalleled joy and victory come from allowing Christ to do "the hard thing" with us.

BETH MOORE

Today's Prayer

Dear Lord, today, I will join in the celebration of life. I will be a joyful Christian, and I will share my joy with all those who cross my path. You have given me countless blessings, Lord, and today I will thank You by celebrating my life, my faith, and my Savior. Amen

for girls

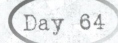

You'd Better Beware

The Lord is pleased with a good person,
but he will punish anyone who plans evil.
PROVERBS 12:2 NCV

Face facts: this world is inhabited by quite a few people who are very determined to do evil things. The devil and his human helpers are working 24/7 to cause pain and heartbreak in every corner of the globe . . . including your corner. So you'd better beware.

Your job, if you choose to accept it, is to recognize evil and fight it. The moment that you decide to fight evil whenever you see it, you can no longer be a lukewarm, halfhearted Christian. And, when you are no longer a lukewarm Christian, God rejoices while the devil despairs.

When will you choose to get serious about fighting the evils of our world? Before you answer that question, consider this: in the battle of good versus evil, the devil never takes a day off . . . and neither should you.

more stuff to think about

Light is stronger than darkness—darkness cannot "comprehend" or "overcome" it.

ANNE GRAHAM LOTZ

Where God's ministers are most successful, there the powers of darkness marshal their forces for the conflict.

LOTTIE MOON

Today's Prayer

Dear Lord, sometimes people are cruel. Let me never be such a person. Let me treat others as I wish to be treated, and let my thoughts and actions honor You today and forever. Amen

for girls

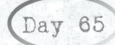

Peer Pressure 101

We must obey God rather than men.
ACTS 5:29 HCSB

Peer pressure can be good or bad, depending upon who your peers are and how they behave. If your friends encourage you to follow God's will and to obey His commandments, then you'll experience positive peer pressure, and that's a good thing. But, if your friends encourage you to do foolish things, then you're facing a different kind of peer pressure . . . and you'd better beware. When you feel pressured to do things—or to say things— that lead you away from God, you're heading straight for trouble. So don't do the "easy" thing or the "popular" thing. Do the right thing, and don't worry about winning any popularity contests.

Are you satisfied to follow the crowd? If so, you will probably pay a heavy price for your shortsightedness. But if you're determined to follow the One from Galilee, He will guide your steps and bless your undertakings. To sum it up, here's your choice: you can choose to please God first, or you can fall victim to peer pressure. The choice is yours— and so are the consequences.

more stuff to think about

Do you want to be wise? Choose wise friends.

CHARLES SWINDOLL

You will get untold flak for prioritizing God's revealed and
present will for your life over man's . . .
but, boy, is it worth it.

BETH MOORE

Today's Prayer

Dear Lord, other people may encourage me to stray from Your path, but I wish to follow in the footsteps of Your Son. Give me the vision to see the right path—and the wisdom to follow it—today and every day of my life. Amen

for girls

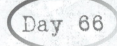

You and Your Family

Unless the Lord builds the house,
They labor in vain who build it; Unless the Lord guards
the city, The watchman stays awake in vain.

PSALM 127:1 NKJV

A loving family is a treasure from God. If God has blessed you with a close-knit, supportive clan, offer a word of thanks to your Creator because He has given you one of His most precious earthy possessions. Your obligation, in response to God's gift, is to treat your family in ways that are consistent with His commandments.

You live in a fast-paced, demanding world; a place where life can be difficult and pressures can be intense. As those pressures build, you may tend to focus so intently upon your obligations that you lose sight, albeit temporarily, of your spiritual and emotional needs (that's one reason why a regular daily devotional time is so important; it offers a badly-needed dose of perspective).

So the next time your family life becomes a little stressful, remember this: That little band of men, women, kids, and babies is a priceless treasure on temporary loan from the Father above. And it's your responsibility to praise God for that gift—and to act accordingly.

more stuff to think about

For whatever life holds for you and your family in the coming
days, weave the unfailing fabric of God's Word through
your heart and mind. It will hold strong,
even if the rest of life unravels.

GIGI GRAHAM TCHIVIDJIAN

There is so much compassion and understanding
that is gained when we've experienced God's grace
firsthand within our own families.

LISA WHELCHEL

Today's Prayer

Lord, You have given me a family that cares for me
and loves me. Thank You, Father. Let me love all the
members of my family despite their imperfections, and
let them love me despite mine. Amen

for girls

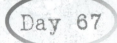

Fully Grown?

*Grow in grace and understanding of our Master and Savior,
Jesus Christ. Glory to the Master, now and forever! Yes!*

2 PETER 3:18 MSG

Are you a fully-grown girl? Physically: maybe so. But spiritually? No way! And thank goodness that you're not! Even if you're a very mature person—even if you're a righteous, spiritual, godly woman—you've still got lots of room to grow.

The 19th-century writer Hannah Whitall Smith observed, "The maturity of a Christian experience cannot be reached in a moment." No kidding. In truth, the search for spiritual growth lasts a lifetime.

When we cease to grow, either emotionally or spiritually, we do ourselves and our families a profound disservice. But, if we study God's Word, if we obey His commandments, and if we live in the center of His will, we will not be "stagnant" believers; we will, instead, be growing Christians . . . and that's exactly what God wants for our lives. Come to think of it, that's exactly what you should want, too.

more stuff to think about

There is wonderful freedom and joy in coming to recognize
that the fun is in the becoming.

GLORIA GAITHER

Kindness in this world will do much to help others,
not only to come into the light,
but also to grow in grace day by day.

FANNY CROSBY

Today's Prayer

Dear Lord, the Bible tells me that You are at work in my
life, continuing to help me grow and to mature in my
faith. Show me Your wisdom, Father, and let me live
according to Your Word and Your will. Amen

for girls

Controlling Your Temper

My dear brothers and sisters, be quick to listen, slow to speak, and slow to get angry.
Your anger can never make things right in God's sight.

JAMES 1:19-20 NLT

Temper tantrums are usually unproductive, unattractive, unforgettable, and unnecessary. Perhaps that's why Proverbs 16:32 states that, "Controlling your temper is better than capturing a city" (NCV).

If you've allowed anger to become a regular visitor at your house, you should pray for wisdom, for patience, and for a heart that is so filled with forgiveness that it contains no room for bitterness. God will help you terminate your tantrums if you ask Him to—and that's a good thing because anger and peace cannot coexist in the same mind.

If you permit yourself to throw too many tantrums, you will forfeit—at least for now—the peace that might otherwise be yours through Christ. So obey God's Word by turning away from anger today and every day. You'll be glad you did, and so will your family and friends.

more stuff to think about

Life is too short to spend it being angry, bored, or dull.

Anger unresolved will only bring you woe.

Today's Prayer

Lord, when I become angry, help me to remember that You offer me peace. Let me turn to You for wisdom, for patience, and for the peace that only You can give. Amen

for girls

He's Here

Draw close to God, and God will draw close to you.
JAMES 4:8 NLT

D o you ever wonder if God really hears your prayers? If so, you're in good company: lots of very faithful Christians have wondered the same thing. In fact, some of the biggest heroes in the Bible had their doubts— and so, perhaps, will you. But when you have your doubts, remember this: God isn't on vacation, and He hasn't moved out of town. God isn't taking a coffee break, and He isn't snoozing on the couch. He's right here, right now, listening to your thoughts and prayers, watching over your every move.

As the demands of everyday life weigh down upon you, you may be tempted to ignore God's presence or—worse yet—to rebel against His commandments. But, when you quiet yourself and acknowledge His presence, God touches your heart and restores your spirits. So why not let Him do it right now?

more stuff to think about

If your heart has grown cold, it is because you have moved
away from the fire of His presence.

BETH MOORE

Our souls were made to live in an upper atmosphere,
and we stifle and choke if we live on any lower level.
Our eyes were made to look off from these heavenly heights,
and our vision is distorted by any lower gazing.

HANNAH WHITALL SMITH

Today's Prayer

Dear Lord, You are with me when I am strong and when
I am weak. You never leave my side, even when it seems
to me that You are far away. Today and every day, let
me trust Your promises and let me feel Your love. Amen

for girls

Whose Expectations?

*My dear friends, don't let public opinion influence how you
live out our glorious, Christ-originated faith.*
JAMES 2:1 MSG

Expectations, expectations, expectations! As a young
woman living in the 21st century, you know that
demands can be high, and expectations even higher.
The media delivers an endless stream of messages that tell
you how to look, how to behave, how to eat, and how to
dress. The media's expectations are impossible to meet—
God's are not. God doesn't expect you to be perfect . . .
and neither should you.

Remember: the expectations that really matter are God's
expectations. Everything else takes a back seat. So do your
best to please God, and don't worry too much about what
other people think. And, when it comes to meeting the
unrealistic expectations of a world gone nuts, forget about
trying to be perfect—it's impossible.

more stuff to think about

It is comfortable to know that we are responsible to God and not to man. It is a small matter to be judged of man's judgement.

LOTTIE MOON

If you try to be everything to everybody, you will end up being nothing to anybody.

VANCE HAVNER

Today's Prayer

Lord, this world has so many expectations of me, but today I will not seek to meet the world's expectations; I will do my best to meet Your expectations. I will make You my ultimate priority, Lord, by serving You, by praising You, by loving You, and by obeying You. Amen

for girls

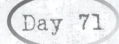

Day 71

Questions, Questions, Questions

Now if any of you lacks wisdom, he should ask God,
who gives to all generously and without criticizing,
and it will be given to him. But let him ask in faith without
doubting. For the doubter is like the surging sea,
driven and tossed by the wind.

JAMES 1:5-6 HCSB

So many questions and so few answers! If that statement seems to describe the current state of your spiritual life, don't panic. Even the most faithful Christians are overcome by occasional bouts of fear and doubt. You are no different.

When you feel that your faith is being tested to its limits, seek the comfort and assurance of the One who sent His Son as a sacrifice for you. And remember: Even when you feel very distant from God, God is never distant from you. When you sincerely seek His presence, He will touch your heart, calm your fears, and restore your soul.

2 MINUTES A DAY

more stuff to think about

When there is perplexity there is always guidance—
not always at the moment we ask, but in good time,
which is God's time. There is no need to fret and stew.

ELISABETH ELLIOT

We are finding we don't have such a gnawing need to know
the answers when we know the Answer.

GLORIA GAITHER

Today's Prayer

Dear God, sometimes this world can be a puzzling
place. When I am unsure of my next step, keep me
aware that You are always near. Give me faith, Father,
and let me remember that with Your love and Your
power, I can live courageously and faithfully today
and every day. Amen

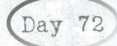

His Commandments

Teach me Your way, O LORD; I will walk in Your truth.
PSALM 86:11 NASB

God gave us His commandments for a reason: so that we might obey them and be blessed. Elisabeth Elliot advised, "Obedience to God is our job. The results of that obedience are God's." These words should serve to remind us that obedience is imperative. But, we live in a world that presents us with countless temptations to disobey God's laws.

When we stray from God's path, we suffer. So, whenever we are confronted with sin, we have clear instructions: we must walk—or better yet run—in the opposite direction.

more stuff to think about

Don't worry about what you do not understand.
Worry about what you do understand in
the Bible but do not live by.

CORRIE TEN BOOM

Only grief and disappointment can result from continued
violation of the divine principles that
underlie the spiritual life.

A. W. TOZER

Today's Prayer

Thank You, Dear Lord, for loving me enough to give me
rules to live by. Let me live by Your commandments,
and let me lead others to do the same. Let me walk
righteously in Your way, Dear Lord, this day and
every day. Amen

for girls

Your Noisy World

Be still before the Lord and wait patiently for Him.
PSALM 37:7 NIV

Face it: We live in a noisy world, a world filled with distractions, frustrations, and complications. But if we allow those distractions to separate us from God's peace, we do ourselves a profound disservice.

Are you one of those busy girls who rush through the day with scarcely a single moment for quiet contemplation and prayer? If so, it's time to reorder your priorities.

Nothing is more important than the time you spend with your Savior. So be still and claim the inner peace that is your spiritual birthright: the peace of Jesus Christ. It is offered freely; it has been paid for in full; it is yours for the asking. So ask. And then share.

more stuff to think about

The manifold rewards of a serious, consistent prayer life demonstrate clearly that time with our Lord should be our first priority.

SHIRLEY DOBSON

Jesus taught us by example to get out of the rat race and recharge our batteries.

BARBARA JOHNSON

Today's Prayer

Lord, Your Holy Word is a light unto the world; let me study it, trust it, and share it with all who cross my path. Let me discover You, Father, in the quiet moments of the day. And, in all that I say and do, help me to be a worthy witness as I share the Good News of Your perfect Son and Your perfect Word. Amen

for girls

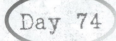

When Mistakes Are Made

*Therefore, if anyone is in Christ, he is a new creation;
the old has gone, the new has come!*

2 Corinthians 5:17 NIV

Mistakes: nobody likes 'em but everybody makes 'em. Sometimes, even if you're a very good person, you're going to mess things up. And when you do, God is always ready to forgive you—He'll do His part, but you should be willing to do your part, too. Here's what you need to do:

1. If you've been engaging in behavior that is against the will of God, cease and desist (that means stop). 2. If you made a mistake, learn from it and don't repeat it (that's called getting smarter). 3. If you've hurt somebody, apologize and ask for forgiveness (that's called doing the right thing). Have you made a mistake? If so, today is the perfect day to make things right with everybody (and the word "everybody" includes yourself, your family, your friends, and your God).

Mistakes are the price you pay for being human; repeated mistakes are the price you pay for being stubborn. So don't be hardheaded: learn from your experiences—the first time!

more stuff to think about

Father, take our mistakes and turn them into opportunities.

MAX LUCADO

If at first you don't succeed, read the Instruction Manual—
God's.

ANONYMOUS

Today's Prayer

Lord, sometimes I make mistakes and fall short of
Your commandments. When I do, forgive me, Father.
And help me learn from my mistakes so that I can
be a better servant to You and a better example to my
friends and family. Amen

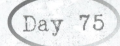

Day 75

Wise Yet?

*Do you want to be counted wise, to build a reputation
for wisdom? Here's what you do: Live well, live wisely,
live humbly. It's the way you live,
not the way you talk, that counts.*

JAMES 3:13 MSG

All of us would like to be wise, but not all of us are willing to do the work that is required to become wise. Why? Because wisdom isn't free—it takes time and effort to acquire.

To become wise, we must seek God's wisdom and live according to His Word. To become wise, we must seek wisdom with consistency and purpose. To become wise, we must not only learn the lessons of the Christian life, we must also live by them.

If you sincerely desire to become wise—and if you seek to share your hard-earned wisdom with others—your actions must give credence to your words. The best way to share one's wisdom—perhaps the only way—is not by words, but by example.

Wisdom is like a savings account: If you add to it consistently, then eventually you'll have a great sum. The secret to success is consistency. Do you seek wisdom? Then seek it every day, and seek it in the right place. That place, of course, is, first and foremost, the Word of God.

more stuff to think about

No matter how many books you read,
no matter how many schools you attend, you're never really
wise until you start making wise choices.

MARIE T. FREEMAN.

Wisdom is knowledge applied.
Head knowledge is useless on the battlefield.
Knowledge stamped on the heart makes one wise.

BETH MOORE

Today's Prayer

Lord, when I trust in the wisdom of the world, I will
sometimes be led astray, but when I trust in Your
wisdom, I build my life on a firm foundation. Today
and every day I will trust Your Word and follow it,
knowing that the ultimate wisdom is Your wisdom and
the ultimate truth is Your truth. Amen

for girls

The Hem of His Garment

*Now faith is being sure of what we hope for
and certain of what we do not see.*

HEBREWS 11:1 NIV

Concentration camp survivor Corrie ten Boom relied on faith during ten months of imprisonment and torture. Later, despite the fact that four of her family members had died in Nazi death camps, Corrie's faith was unshaken. She wrote, "There is no pit so deep that God's love is not deeper still." Christians take note: Genuine faith in God means faith in all circumstances, happy or sad, joyful or tragic.

When you place your faith, your trust, indeed your life in the hands of Christ Jesus, you'll be amazed at the marvelous things He can do with you and through you. So strengthen your faith through praise, through worship, through Bible study, and through prayer. Then, trust God's plans. Your Heavenly Father is standing at the door of your heart. If you reach out to Him in faith, He will give you peace and heal your broken spirit. Be content to touch even the smallest fragment of the Master's garment, and He will make you whole.

more stuff to think about

Faith does not concern itself with the entire journey.
One step is enough.

MRS. CHARLES E. COWMAN

If God chooses to remain silent, faith is content.

RUTH BELL GRAHAM

Today's Prayer

Lord, as I take the next steps on my life's journey, I will take them with You. Because of my faith in You, I can be courageous and strong. I will lean upon You, Father—and trust You—this day and forever. Amen

for girls

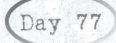

To Shop or Not to Shop?

*No one can serve two masters. The person will hate
one master and love the other, or will follow one master
and refuse to follow the other. You cannot serve
both God and worldly riches.*

MATTHEW 6:24 NCV

Our society is in love with money and the things that money can buy. God is not. God cares about people, not possessions, and so must we. We must, to the best of our abilities, love our neighbors as ourselves, and we must, to the best of our abilities, resist the mighty temptation to place possessions ahead of people.

How much stuff is too much stuff? Well, if your desire for stuff is getting in the way of your desire to know God, then you've got too much stuff—it's as simple as that.

If you find yourself wrapped up in the concerns of the material world, it's time to reorder your priorities by turning your thoughts to more important matters. And, it's time to begin storing up riches that will endure throughout eternity: the spiritual kind. Money, in and of itself, is not evil; worshipping money is. So today, as you prioritize matters of importance in your life, remember that God is almighty, but the dollar is not.

more stuff to think about

We own too many things that aren't worth owning.

MARIE T. FREEMAN

As faithful stewards of what we have, ought we not to give
earnest thought to our staggering surplus?

ELISABETH ELLIOT

Today's Prayer

Dear Lord, Keep me mindful that material possessions
cannot bring me joy—my joy comes from You. I will
share that joy with family, with friends, and with
neighbors, this day and every day. Amen

for girls

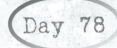

Day 78

Doing It Now

Lazy farmers don't plow when they should;
they expect a harvest, but there is none.
PROVERBS 20:4 NCV

When something important needs to be done, the best time to do it is sooner rather than later. But sometimes, instead of doing the smart thing (which, by the way, is choosing "sooner"), we may choose "later." When we do, we may pay a heavy price for our shortsightedness.

Are you one of those people who puts things off till the last minute? If so, it's time to change you ways. Your procrastination is probably the result of your shortsighted attempt to postpone (or avoid altogether) the discomfort that you associate with a particular activity. Get over it!

Whatever "it" is, do it now. When you do, you won't have to worry about "it" later.

2 Minutes A Day

more stuff to think about

Do noble things, do not dream them all day long.

CHARLES KINGSLEY

I cannot fix what I will not face.

JIM GALLERY

Today's Prayer

Dear Lord, today is a new day. Help me tackle the important tasks immediately, even if those tasks are unpleasant. Don't let me put off until tomorrow what I should do today. Amen

for girls

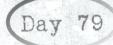

God Can Handle It

*For I, the Lord your God, hold your right hand
and say to you: Do not fear, I will help you.*
ISAIAH 41:13 HCSB

It's a promise that is made over and over again in the
Bible: Whatever "it" is, God can handle it.

Life isn't always easy. Far from it! Sometimes, life can be
very, very tough. But even then, even during our darkest
moments, we're protected by a loving Heavenly Father.
When we're worried, God can reassure us; when we're sad,
God can comfort us. When our hearts are broken, God is
not just near, He is here. So we must lift our thoughts and
prayers to Him. When we do, He will answer our prayers.
Why? Because He is our shepherd, and He has promised to
protect us now and forever.

more stuff to think about

God is always sufficient in perfect proportion to our need.

BETH MOORE

God's saints in all ages have realized that
God was enough for them. God is enough for time;
God is enough for eternity. God is enough!

HANNAH WHITALL SMITH

Today's Prayer

Dear Lord, whatever "it" is, You can handle it! Let me
turn to You when I am fearful or worried. You are my
loving Heavenly Father, sufficient in all things, I will
always trust You. Amen

for girls

You and Your Conscience

So I strive always to keep my conscience
clear before God and man.
ACTS 24:16 NIV

It has been said that character is what we are when nobody is watching. How true. When we do things that we know aren't right, we try to hide them from our families and friends. But even then, God is watching.

Few things in life torment us more than a guilty conscience. And, few things in life provide more contentment than the knowledge that we are obeying the conscience that God has placed in our hearts.

If you sincerely want to create the best possible life for yourself and your loved ones, never forsake your conscience. And remember this: when you walk with God, your character will take care of itself...and you won't need to look over your shoulder to see who, besides God, is watching.

more stuff to think about

God desires that we become spiritually healthy enough
through faith to have a conscience that rightly interprets
the work of the Holy Spirit.

BETH MOORE

If I am walking along the street with a very disfiguring hole
in the back of my dress, of which I am in ignorance,
it is certainly a very great comfort to me to have a kind friend
who will tell me of it. And similarly, it is indeed a comfort
to know that there is always abiding with me a divine,
all-seeing Comforter, who will reprove me for all my faults
and will not let me go on in a fatal unconsciousness of them.

HANNAH WHITALL SMITH

Today's Prayer

Lord, You have given me a conscience that tells me
right from wrong. Let me listen to that quiet voice so
that I might do Your will and follow Your Word today
and every day. Amen

for girls

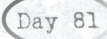

Beyond Discouragement

But as for you, be strong; don't be discouraged,
for your work has a reward.

2 Chronicles 15:7 HCSB

We Christians have many reasons to celebrate. God is in His heaven; Christ has risen, and we are the sheep of His flock. Yet sometimes, even the most devout Christian women can become discouraged. After all, we live in a world where expectations can be high and demands can be even higher. If you become discouraged with the direction of your day or your life, turn your thoughts and prayers to God. He is a God of possibility, not negativity. He will help you count your blessings instead of your hardships. And then, with a renewed spirit of optimism and hope, you can properly thank your Father in heaven for His blessings, for His love, and for His Son.

more stuff to think about

Overcoming discouragement is simply a matter of taking away the DIS and adding the EN.

BARBARA JOHNSON

Working in the vineyard,
Working all the day,
Never be discouraged,
Only watch and pray.

FANNY CROSBY

Today's Prayer

Heavenly Father, when I am discouraged, I will turn to You, and I will also turn to my Christian friends. I Thank You, Father, for friends and family members who are willing to encourage me. I will acknowledge their encouragement, and I will share it. Amen

for girls

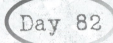

The Gift of Eternal Life

*For God so loved the world that he gave his only Son,
so that everyone who believes in him will not perish
but have eternal life.*

JOHN 3:16 NLT

Your ability to envision the future, like your life here on earth, is limited. God's vision, however, is not burdened by any such limitations. He sees all things, He knows all things, and His plans for you endure for all time.

God's plans are not limited to the events of life-here-on-earth. Your Heavenly Father has bigger things in mind for you . . . much bigger things. So praise the Creator for the gift of eternal life and share the Good News with all who cross your path. You have given your heart to the Son, so you belong to the Father—today, tomorrow, and for all eternity.

2 minutes A DAY

more stuff to think about

The gift of God is eternal life, spiritual life, abundant life through faith in Jesus Christ, the Living Word of God.

ANNE GRAHAM LOTZ

If you are a believer, your judgment will not determine your eternal destiny. Christ's finished work on Calvary was applied to you the moment you accepted Christ as Savior.

BETH MOORE

Today's Prayer

Lord, You have given me the gift of eternal life through Christ Jesus. I praise You for that priceless gift. Because I am saved, I will share the story of Your Son and the glory of my salvation with a world that desperately needs Your grace. Amen

for girls

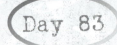

Day 83

Forgiveness Now

Be gentle with one another, sensitive. Forgive one another as quickly and thoroughly as God in Christ forgave you.

EPHESIANS 4:32 MSG

A re you the kind of girl who has a tough time forgiving and forgetting? If so, welcome to the club. Most of us find it difficult to forgive the people who have hurt us. And that's too bad because life would be much simpler if we could forgive people "once and for all" and be done with it. Yet forgiveness is seldom that easy. Usually, the decision to forgive is straightforward, but the process of forgiving is more difficult. Forgiveness is a journey that requires effort, time, perseverance, and prayer.

If there exists even one person whom you have not forgiven (and that includes yourself), obey God's commandment: forgive that person today. And remember that bitterness, anger, and regret are not part of God's plan for your life. Forgiveness is.

If you sincerely wish to forgive someone, pray for that person. And then pray for yourself by asking God to heal your heart. Don't expect forgiveness to be easy or quick, but rest assured: with God as your partner, you can forgive . . . and you will.

2 MINUTES A DAY

more stuff to think about

God expects us to forgive others as He has forgiven us;
we are to follow His example by having a forgiving heart.

Forgiveness is the precondition of love.

CATHERINE MARSHALL

Today's Prayer

Lord, just as You have forgiven me, I am going to
forgive others. When I forgive others, I not only obey
Your commandments, but I also free myself from
bitterness and regret. Forgiveness is Your way, Lord,
and I will make it my way, too. Amen

for girls

Fitness Matters

Whatever you eat or drink or whatever you do,
you must do all for the glory of God.

1 CORINTHIANS 10:31 NLT

A re you shaping up or spreading out? Do you eat sensibly and exercise regularly, or do you spend most of your time on the couch with a Twinkie in one hand and a clicker in the other? Are you choosing to treat your body like a temple or a trash heap? How you answer these questions will help determine how long you live and how well you live.

Physical fitness is a choice, a choice that requires discipline—it's as simple as that. So, do yourself this favor: treat your body like a one-of-a-kind gift from God . . . because that's precisely what your body is.

more stuff to think about

Our primary motivation should not be for more energy
or to avoid a heart attack but to please God with our bodies.

CAROLE LEWIS

God wants you to give Him your body.
Some people do foolish things with their bodies.
God wants your body as a holy sacrifice.

WARREN WIERSBE

Today's Prayer

Lord, all that I am belongs to You. As I serve You with
all that I am and all that I have, help me to honor You
by caring for the body that You have given me. Amen

for girls

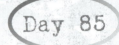

Patience NOW!

*Patient people have great understanding,
but people with quick tempers show their foolishness.*
PROVERBS 14:29 NCV

Most of us are impatient for God to grant us the things that we wish for and hope for. But God may have other plans. And when God's plans differ from our own, we know that we should trust in His infinite wisdom and in His infinite love . . . but we also know from firsthand experience that trusting God is hard to do.

As busy girls living in a fast-paced world, many of us find that waiting quietly for God is difficult. Why? Two reasons: 1. Because we live in a rapidly changing world, we're accustomed to things happening fast. 2. Because we're imperfect human beings, we want to live according to our own timetables, not God's.

God's Word makes it clear: He instructs us to be patient, very patient. We must be patient with our families, with our friends, and with our acquaintances. We must also be patient with our Heavenly Father as He unfolds His plan for our lives. And that's as it should be. After all, think how patient God has been with us.

more stuff to think about

Let me encourage you to continue to wait with faith.
God may not perform a miracle, but He is trustworthy
to touch you and make you whole
where there used to be a hole.

LISA WHELCHEL

He makes us wait. He keeps us in the dark on purpose.
He makes us walk when we want to run, sit still when
we want to walk, for he has things to do in our souls
that we are not interested in.

ELISABETH ELLIOT

Today's Prayer

Lord, sometimes I can be a very impatient person. Slow
me down and calm me down. Let me trust in Your
plan, Father; let me trust in Your timetable; and let me
trust in Your love for me. Amen

for girls

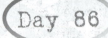

When You Have Doubts

If you don't know what you're doing, pray to the Father.
He loves to help. You'll get his help, and won't be
condescended to when you ask for it. Ask boldly, believingly,
without a second thought. People who "worry their prayers"
are like wind-whipped waves. Don't think you're going to get
anything from the Master that way, adrift at sea,
keeping all your options open.

JAMES 1:5-8 MSG

If you've never had any doubts about your faith, then you can stop reading this page now and skip to the next. But if you've ever been plagued by doubts about your faith or your God, keep reading.

Even some of the most faithful Christians are, at times, beset by occasional bouts of discouragement and doubt. But even when we feel far removed from God, God is never far removed from us. He is always with us, always willing to calm the storms of life—always willing to replace our doubts with comfort and assurance.

Whenever you're plagued by doubts, that's precisely the moment you should seek God's presence by genuinely seeking to establish a deeper, more meaningful relationship with His Son. Then you may rest assured that in time, God will calm your fears, answer your prayers, and restore your confidence.

more stuff to think about

We are most vulnerable to the piercing winds of doubt
when we distance ourselves from the mission
and fellowship to which Christ has called us.

JONI EARECKSON TADA

Fear and doubt are conquered by a faith that rejoices.
And faith can rejoice because the promises of
God are as certain as God Himself.

KAY ARTHUR

Today's Prayer

Dear Lord, when I am filled with uncertainty and
doubt, give me faith. In the dark moments of life, keep
me mindful of Your healing power and Your infinite
love, so that I may live courageously and faithfully
today and every day. Amen

for girls

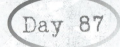

Time for Fun

So I recommend having fun, because there is nothing better for people to do in this world than to eat, drink, and enjoy life. That way they will experience some happiness along with all the hard work God gives them.

ECCLESIASTES 8:15 NLT

Are you a girl who takes time each day to really enjoy life? Hopefully so. After all, you are the recipient of a precious gift—the gift of life. And because God has seen fit to give you this gift, it is incumbent upon you to use it and to enjoy it. But sometimes, amid the inevitable pressures of everyday living, really enjoying life may seem almost impossible. It is not.

For most of us, fun is as much a function of attitude as it is a function of environment. So whether you're standing victorious atop one of life's mountains or trudging through one of life's valleys, enjoy yourself. You deserve to have fun today, and God wants you to have fun today . . . so what on earth are you waiting for?

Our thoughts, not our circumstances,
determine our happiness.

JOHN MAXWELL

I became aware of one very important concept
I had missed before: my attitude—not my circumstances—
was what was making me unhappy.

VONETTE BRIGHT

Today's Prayer

Lord, make me a happy Christian. Let me rejoice in the
gift of this day, and let me praise You for the gift of
Your Son. Make me be a joyful person, Lord, as I share
Your Good News with all those who need Your healing
touch. Amen

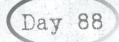

The Dating Game

*Be kindly affectionate to one another with brotherly love,
in honor giving preference to one another; not lagging in
diligence, fervent in spirit, serving the Lord; rejoicing in hope,
patient in tribulation, continuing steadfastly in prayer.*

Romans 12:10–12 NKJV

If you're still searching for Mr. Right (while trying to avoid falling in love with Mr. Wrong), be patient, be prudent, and be picky. Look for a guy whose values you respect, whose behavior you approve of, and whose faith you admire. Remember that appearances can be deceiving and tempting, so watch your step. And when it comes to the important task of building a lifetime relationship with the guy of your dreams, pray about it!

If you happen to be one of those very lucky girls who has already fallen madly in love with the same wonderful guy who has (coincidentally) already fallen madly in love with you, say a great big thanks to the Matchmaker in heaven. But if you haven't yet found Mr. Right, don't fret. Just keep trusting God, and keep yourself open to the direction in which He is leading you. And remember: When if comes to selecting a man, God wants to give His approval—or not—but He won't give it until He's asked. So ask, listen, and decide accordingly.

more stuff to think about

Living life with a consistent spiritual walk deeply influences those we love most.

VONETTE BRIGHT

Love always means sacrifice.

ELISABETH ELLIOT

Today's Prayer

Lord, I will let You rule over every aspect of my life, including my relationships. And I know that when I do, You will help me make choices that are right for me, today and every day that I live. Amen

for girls

Living Courageously

*Do not be afraid or discouraged, for the LORD is
the one who goes before you. He will be with you;
he will neither fail you nor forsake you.*

Deuteronomy 31:8 NLT

Christian women have every reason to live courageously. After all, the final battle has already been won on the cross at Calvary. But even dedicated followers of Christ may find their courage tested by the inevitable disappointments and fears that visit the lives of believers and non-believers alike.

When you find yourself worried about the challenges of today or the uncertainties of tomorrow, you must ask yourself whether or not you are ready to place your concerns and your life in God's all-powerful, all-knowing, all-loving hands. If the answer to that question is yes—as it should be—then you can draw courage today from the source of strength that never fails: your Heavenly Father.

2 MINUTES A DAY

more stuff to think about

If a person fears God, he or she has no reason to fear anything else. On the other hand, if a person does not fear God, then fear becomes a way of life.

BETH MOORE

When once we are assured that God is good, then there can be nothing left to fear.

HANNAH WHITALL SMITH

Today's Prayer

Lord, I'm only human, and sometimes I am afraid. But You are always with me, and when I turn to You, You give me courage. Let me be a courageous, faith-filled Christian, God, and keep me mindful that, with You as my protector, I am secure today . . . and throughout eternity. Amen

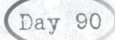

Running on Empty

I will give you a new heart and put a new spirit in you....
EZEKIEL 36:26 NIV

For an extremely busy girl living in an extremely busy world, life may seem like a merry-go-round that never stops turning. If that description fits you, then you may find yourself running short of patience, or strength, or both. If you're feeling exhausted or discouraged, there is a source from which you can draw the power needed to recharge your spiritual batteries. That source is God.

Are you tired or troubled? Turn your heart toward God in prayer. Are you weak or worried? Take the time—or, more accurately, make the time—to study God's Word. Do you feel like your emotional resources are almost gone? Call upon fellow believers to support you, and call upon Christ to renew your spirit and your life. When you do, you'll discover that the Creator of the universe can make everything new, including you.

more stuff to think about

He is the God of wholeness and restoration.

STORMIE OMARTIAN

If you're willing to repair your life, God is willing to help.
If you're not willing to repair your life,
God is willing to wait.

MARIE T. FREEMAN

Today's Prayer

Heavenly Father, sometimes I am troubled, and
sometimes I grow weary. When I am weak, Lord, give
me strength. When I am discouraged, renew me. When
I am fearful, let me feel Your healing touch. Let me
always trust in Your promises, Lord, and let me draw
strength from those promises and from Your unending
love. Amen

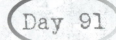

Day 91

The Wisdom to be Generous

Freely you have received, freely give.

MATTHEW 10:8 NIV

God's gifts are beyond description, His blessings beyond comprehension. God has been incredibly generous with us, and He rightfully expects us to be generous with others. That's why the thread of generosity is woven into the very fabric of God's teachings.

In the Old Testament, we are told that, "The good person is generous and lends lavishly…." (Psalm 112:5 MSG). And in the New Testament we are instructed, "Freely you have received, freely give" (Matthew 10:8 NKJV). These principles still apply. As we establish priorities for our days and our lives, we are advised to give freely of our time, our possessions, and our love—just as God has given freely to us.

Of course, we can never fully repay God for His gifts, but we can share them with others. And we should.

more stuff to think about

The measure of a life, after all, is not its duration
but its donation.

CORRIE TEN BOOM

Nothing is really ours until we share it.

C. S. LEWIS

Today's Prayer

Lord, make me a generous and cheerful Christian. Let
me be kind to those who need my encouragement, and
let me share with those who need my help, today and
every day. Amen

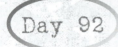

Radical Faith

I've laid down a pattern for you. What I've done, you do.
JOHN 13:15 MSG

When it comes to your faith, are you "radical" or "run-of-the-mill"? Is your life radically different because of your relationship with Jesus, or are you the same person you were before you invited Him into your life?

Jesus wants to have a radical, life-altering relationship with you. Are you willing to have a radical relationship with Him? Unless you can answer this question with a resounding "Yes," you will rob yourself of the abundance that can and should be yours through Christ.

Ruth Bell Graham observed, "God's work is not in buildings, but in transformed lives." Are you a transformed person because of your relationship with the One from Galilee? Hopefully so. When you invited Christ to reign over your heart, you become a radically new creation. This day offers yet another opportunity to behave yourself like that new person. When you do, God will guide your steps and bless your endeavors . . . forever.

more stuff to think about

Jesus challenges you and me to keep our focus daily
on the cross of His will if we want to be His disciples.

It's your heart that Jesus longs for: your will to be made
His own with self on the cross forever,
and Jesus alone on the throne.

RUTH BELL GRAHAM

Today's Prayer

Dear Lord, You sent Jesus to save the world and to save
me. I thank You for Jesus, and I will do my best to
follow Him, today and forever. Amen

for girls

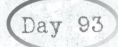

Richly Blessed

Blessings are on the head of the righteous.
PROVERBS 10:6 HCSB

Have you counted your blessings lately? You should. Of course, God's gifts are too numerous to count, but as a grateful Christian, you should attempt to count them nonetheless.

Your blessings include life, family, friends, talents, and possessions, for starters. And your greatest gift—a treasure that was paid for on the cross and is yours for the asking—is God's gift of salvation through Christ Jesus.

As believing Christians, we have all been blessed beyond measure. Thus, thanksgiving should become a habit, a regular part of our daily routines. Today, let us pause and thank our Creator for His blessings. And let us demonstrate our gratitude to the Giver of all things good by using His gifts for the glory of His kingdom.

more stuff to think about

God is always far more willing to give us good things
than we are anxious to have them.

CATHERINE MARSHALL

The Christian life is motivated, not by a list of do's
and don'ts, but by the gracious outpouring of
God's love and blessing.

ANNE GRAHAM LOTZ

Today's Prayer

Today, Lord, let me count my blessings with
thanksgiving in my heart. You have cared for me,
Lord, and I will give You the glory and the praise. Let
me accept Your blessings and Your gifts, and let me
share them with others, just as You first shared them
with me. Amen

for girls

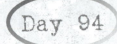

God's Guidance

*The LORD says, "I will guide you along the best pathway for
your life. I will advise you and watch over you."*

PSALM 32:8 NLT

The Bible promises that God will guide you if you let
Him. Your job, of course, is to let Him. But sometimes,
you will be tempted to do otherwise. Sometimes, you'll
be tempted to go along with the crowd; other times, you'll
be tempted to do things your way, not God's way. When you
feel those temptations, resist them.

What will you allow to guide you through the coming
day: your own desires (or, for that matter, the desires of
your friends)? Or will you allow God to lead the way? The
answer should be obvious. You should let God be your
guide. When you entrust your life to Him completely and
without reservation, God will give you the strength to meet
any challenge, the courage to face any trial, and the wisdom
to live in His righteousness. So trust Him today and seek His
guidance. When you do, your next step will be the right one.

more stuff to think about

If we neglect the Bible, we cannot expect to benefit from
the wisdom and direction that result from
knowing God's Word.

VONETTE BRIGHT

It is a joy that God never abandons His children.
He guides faithfully all who listen to His directions.

CORRIE TEN BOOM

Today's Prayer

Dear Lord, today I will trust You more completely. I
will lean upon Your understanding, not mine. And I
will trust You to guide my steps along a path of Your
choosing. Amen

for girls

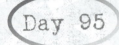

Too Busy?

Careful planning puts you ahead in the long run;
hurry and scurry puts you further behind.

PROVERBS 21:5 MSG

Everybody knows you're a very busy girl. But here's a question: are you able to squeeze time into your hectic schedule for God? Hopefully so! But if you're one of those girls who rush through the day with scarcely a single moment to talk with your Creator, it's time to reshuffle your priorities.

You live in a noisy world, a world filled with distractions, frustrations, temptations, and complications. But if you allow the distractions of everyday life to distract you from God's peace, you're doing yourself a big disservice. So here's some good advice: instead of rushing nonstop through the day, slow yourself down long enough to have a few quiet minutes with God.

Nothing is more important than the time you spend with your Heavenly Father. Absolutely nothing. So be still and claim the inner peace that is your spiritual birthright: the peace of Jesus Christ. It is offered freely; it has been paid for in full; it is yours for the asking. So ask. And then share.

more stuff to think about

The demand of every day kept me so busy
that I subconsciously equated my busyness
with commitment to Christ.

VONETTE BRIGHT

Frustration is not the will of God. There is time to do
anything and everything that God wants us to do.

ELISABETH ELLIOT

Today's Prayer

Dear Lord, sometimes, I am distracted by the busyness
of the day or the demands of the moment. When I am
worried or anxious, Father, turn my thoughts back
to You. Help me to trust Your will, to follow Your
commands, and to accept Your peace, today and forever.
Amen

for girls

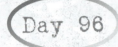

Beyond Guilt

There is therefore now no condemnation to those who are in Christ Jesus, who do not walk according to the flesh, but according to the Spirit.

ROMANS 8:1 NKJV

All of us have made mistakes. Sometimes our failures result from our own shortsightedness. On other occasions, we are swept up in events that are beyond our abilities to control. Under either set of circumstances, we may experience intense feelings of guilt. But God has an answer for the guilt that we feel. That answer, of course, is His forgiveness.

When we ask our Heavenly Father for His forgiveness, He forgives us completely and without reservation. Then, we must do the difficult work of forgiving ourselves in the same way that God has forgiven us: thoroughly and unconditionally.

If you're feeling guilty, then it's time for a special kind of housecleaning—a housecleaning of your mind and your heart . . . beginning NOW!

more stuff to think about

If God has forgiven you, why can't you forgive yourself?

MARIE T. FREEMAN

Satan knows that if you live under a dark cloud of guilt,
you will not be able to witness effectively or
serve the Lord with power and blessing.

WARREN WIERSBE

Today's Prayer

Dear Lord, thank You for the guilt that I feel when I
disobey You. Help me confess my wrongdoings, help
me accept Your forgiveness, and help me renew my
passion to serve You. Amen

for girls

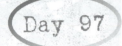
Finding Hope

*May the God of hope fill you with all joy and peace as you
trust in him, so that you may overflow with hope by
the power of the Holy Spirit.*

ROMANS 15:13 NIV

There are few sadder sights on earth than the sight of a
girl or guy who has lost hope. In difficult times, hope
can be elusive, but those who place their faith in God's
promises need never lose it. After all, God is good; His love
endures; He has promised His children the gift of eternal life.
And, God keeps His promises.

If you find yourself falling into the spiritual traps of worry
and discouragement, seek the healing touch of Jesus and
the encouraging words of fellow believers. And if you find a
friend in need, remind him or her of the peace that is found
through a genuine relationship with Christ.

This world can be a place of trials and troubles, but as
believers, we are secure. God has promised us peace, joy,
and eternal life. And, of course, God keeps His promises
today, tomorrow, and forever.

more stuff to think about

Hope must be in the future tense. Faith, to be faith,
must always be in the present tense.

CATHERINE MARSHALL

Love is the seed of all hope. It is the enticement to trust,
to risk, to try, and to go on.

GLORIA GAITHER

Today's Prayer

Today, Dear Lord, I will live in hope. If I become
discouraged, I will turn to You. If I grow weary, I will
seek strength in You. In every aspect of my life, I will
trust You. You are my Father, Lord, and I place my
hope and my faith in You. Amen

for girls

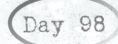
His Joy and Yours

A joyful heart is good medicine,
but a broken spirit dries up the bones.
PROVERBS 17:22 NASB

Have you made the choice to rejoice? Hopefully so. After all, if you're a believer, you have plenty of reasons to be joyful. Yet sometimes, amid the inevitable hustle and bustle of life-here-on-earth, you may lose sight of your blessings as you wrestle with the challenges of everyday life.

Christ made it clear to His followers: He intended that His joy would become their joy. And it still holds true today: Christ intends that His believers share His love with His joy in their hearts.

What does life have in store for you? A world full of possibilities (of course it's up to you to seize them), and God's promise of abundance (of course it's up to you to accept it). So, as you embark upon the next phase of your journey, remember to celebrate the life that God has given you. Your Creator has blessed you beyond measure. Honor Him with your prayers, your words, your deeds, and your joy.

more stuff to think about

Finding joy means first of all finding Jesus.

JILL BRISCOE

What is your focus today? Joy comes when it is Jesus first, others second…then you.

KAY ARTHUR

Today's Prayer

Dear Lord, You have given me so many blessings; let me celebrate Your gifts. Make me thankful, loving, responsible, and wise. I praise You, Father, for the gift of Your Son and for the priceless gift of salvation. Make me be a joyful Christian and a worthy example to my loved ones, today and every day. Amen

for girls

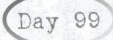

Choosing to be Kind

Our Father is kind; you be kind. "Don't pick on people,
jump on their failures, criticize their faults— unless, of course,
you want the same treatment. Don't condemn those
who are down; that hardness can boomerang.
Be easy on people; you'll find life a lot easier.

Luke 6:36-37 MSG

Kindness is a choice. Sometimes, when we feel happy or generous, we find it easy to be kind. Other times, when we are discouraged or tired, we can scarcely summon the energy to utter a single kind word. But, God's commandment is clear: He intends that we make the conscious choice to treat others with kindness and respect, no matter our circumstances, no matter our emotions.

In the busyness and confusion of daily life, it is easy to lose focus, and it is easy to become frustrated. We are imperfect human beings struggling to manage our lives as best we can, but we often fall short. When we are distracted or disappointed, we may neglect to share a kind word or a kind deed. This oversight hurts others, but it hurts us most of all.

Today, slow yourself down and be alert for people who need your smile, your kind words, or your helping hand. Make kindness a centerpiece of your dealings with others. They will be blessed, and you will be too.

more stuff to think about

Kindness in this world will do much to help others,
not only to come into the light,
but also to grow in grace day by day.

FANNY CROSBY

Sometimes one little spark of kindness is all it takes to
reignite the light of hope in a heart that's blinded by pain.

BARBARA JOHNSON

Today's Prayer

Lord, make me a loving, encouraging Christian. And,
let my love for Christ be reflected through the kindness
that I show to those who need the healing touch of the
Master's hand. Amen

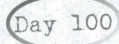

Day 100

Enthused About Life

Whatever you do, work at it with all your heart,
as working for the Lord, not for men.

COLOSSIANS 3:23 NIV

Do you see each day as a glorious opportunity to serve God and to do His will? Are you enthused about life, or do you struggle through each day giving scarcely a thought to God's blessings? Are you constantly praising God for His gifts, and are you sharing His Good News with the world? And are you excited about the possibilities for service that God has placed before you, whether at home, at work, at church, or at school? You should be.

You are the recipient of Christ's sacrificial love. Accept it enthusiastically and share it fervently. Jesus deserves your enthusiasm; the world deserves it; and you deserve the experience of sharing it.

more stuff to think about

Enthusiasm, like the flu, is contagious—
we get it from one another.

BARBARA JOHNSON

Catch on fire with enthusiasm and people will come for
miles to watch you burn.

JOHN WESLEY

Today's Prayer

Dear Lord, let me be an enthusiastic participant in life.
And let my enthusiasm bring honor and glory to You.
Amen

for gi